W9-DEU-411

Themes and Variations
in Community Policing:
Case Studies of Community Policing

Police Executive Research Forum

This publication was supported through grant #90-IJ-CX-K008 from the National Institute of Justice, Office of Justice Programs, U.S. Department of Justice. The points of view expressed herein are the authors' and do not necessarily represent the official position of the U.S. Department of Justice or the opinions of the Police Executive Research Forum's (PERF's) members.

This publication was prepared over a period of time with input from PERF staff, including John Eck, Karin Schmerler, Amy Schapiro, and Deborah Lamm Weisel. The authors of the six case studies contained herein provided valuable insight into the research process, and their participation and their police agencies' contribution of their time are gratefully acknowledged.

Police Executive Research Forum, Washington, D.C. 20036
©1996 by Police Executive Research Forum

All rights reserved

Printed in the United States of America

Library of Congress Catalog Card Number 96-67352

ISBN 1-878734-42-3

Cover by Marnie Deacon

Contents

iv

Introduction

Widespread interest in community policing continues. But whether one reads the extensive literature on the subject or reviews current practices, there is no single articulated form of community policing. Instead, police agencies are engaged in a diverse set of practices united by the general idea that the police and the public need to become better partners to control crime, disorder and a host of other problems. Although numerous police agencies are practicing some form of community policing, little is known about the variations of community policing being practiced.

To address the dearth of information, with funding from the National Institute of Justice, the Police Executive Research Forum (PERF) conducted case studies of community policing in six geographically diverse cities: Edmonton, Alberta, Canada; Newport News, Va.; Las Vegas; Philadelphia; Santa Barbara, Calif.; and Savannah, Ga. The city police agencies were selected on the basis of their self-described participation in community policing and the variation of their approaches to community policing. The agencies, for example, variably focus on problem solving and community engagement activities, conducted through a range of special units and patrol personnel, and in varying locations. The agencies also use varying implementation approaches. Because community policing strategies are so diverse, the research was intended to offer some insight into these varying approaches. The basic research question addressed was, What are police departments actually doing when they say they are doing community policing? Although these case studies were not evaluative in nature, by studying the actual application of community policing, PERF has learned a great deal about the theme and variation of this approach.

The study began with a site selection process in which PERF research staff scrutinized published literature and conducted telephone interviews with knowledgeable academicians, police practitioners and government officials to identify police agencies believed to be substantially engaged in community policing, with some historical basis of experience. There was no perceived benefit in studying agencies that had only recently launched their community policing efforts. PERF then queried the agencies to confirm their participation in community policing and determine their basic approach. On the basis of this information and the agencies' willingness to participate in research, PERF selected six geographically diverse sites for study.

The study continued with a review of attributes and activities thought to be common to community policing. These attributes and activities were used to frame the study and formed the basis for a data collection and interview protocol to be used on-site. This protocol, included as an appendix to this report, included questions about the agencies' context and environment; characteristics and operating style; planning, implementation and management processes used for community policing; collaboration with the community and other agencies; and measures of effectiveness. A standardized protocol was developed to ensure the collection of similar information across sites.

Site visits were conducted in each city, and detailed information was collected on the practice of particular styles of community policing in each. Data were collected through several methods, including review of supporting documentation such as mission and value statements, standard operating procedures and general orders, performance appraisal forms, training materials, and so forth. Interviews were conducted with patrol officers and supervisors engaged in community policing, police managers and police executives, as well as city officials and a limited number of community members.

The site-specific research was carried out by a team of six practitioner-investigators, primarily during a one-week on-site visit, supplemented with follow-up telephone interviews. The police practitioners were Assistant Chief Lynn Babcock, Glendale, Ariz., Police Department; Lt. George Barrett, Louisville, Ky., Police Department; Lt. Ondra

Berry, Reno, Nev., Police Department; Michael Butler, former commander at the Boulder, Colo., Police Department, and now chief of the Longmont, Colo., Police Department; Capt. Carl Hawkins Jr., Hillsborough County Sheriff's Office; and Lt. Jeff Young, Oxnard, Calif., Police Department. Each practitioner was teamed with a member of PERF's research staff. Each two-person team studied one of the community policing sites, preparing a descriptive case study as a product of their work. These case studies constitute the majority of this document.

The teaming of researchers and practitioners is an innovative approach to gathering information designed for final use by police practitioners and others at the local level. This teaming of researchers and practitioners ensures that valid information is collected and questions critical to the research users are addressed. Practitioners were selected who had direct field experience with implementing community policing efforts in their own agency. Thus, their natural inquisitiveness about program objectives and execution had a functional basis that enhanced the theoretical basis of the study. Hence, the sum of this pairing was greater than its parts, for the combined background and experience of researchers and practitioners provided greater insight, balance and practicability in data collection than would otherwise be possible.

Consistency in data collection was obtained through training, use of the standardized interview protocol and significant research guidance. The result is a rich set of programmatic information and descriptions of community policing that are of great use to practitioners. It should be noted that each case study reflects the author's point of view—which is both a contribution and a limitation to the case study methodology. The author decides what information to present and how to organize and present this information. Thus, these cases to some degree reflect author bias. However, every effort has been made to present information in a neutral way that allows the reader to draw his or her own conclusions.

Data for this study were collected during the winter and spring of 1993. The reader should be aware that conditions in the agencies are likely to have changed since the data were originally collected. For example, the Newport News police chief left the agency following the data collection period, a factor that may have significantly changed the face of community policing in that agency. Nonetheless, the information in these case studies was deemed accurate up to the completion of the data collection period in 1993. No effort has been made to make the cases unconditionally current, a status that can be achieved once but never maintained due to the limitations of publication. The reader's recognition of these inherent limitations is an important part of understanding these cases and their contribution to policing.

DEFINING COMMUNITY POLICING

Before examining the following six case studies, the reader is urged to contemplate the range of alternative approaches to community policing. The authors have taken steps to thoroughly describe the historical and organizational context in which community policing emerged in each agency and describe the process through which implementation subsequently occurred. But what types of approaches *could* have been used in each agency? What alternatives were available to police leadership? Why was one approach selected over another? These questions beg consideration by readers. Important to evaluating alternative approaches is a consideration of the range of community policing approaches that may be in current use across the nation. This section provides a brief overview of alternative approaches to and definitions of community policing, providing the reader with a basis for understanding variations in it.

It is difficult to determine precisely how many police agencies are involved in community-oriented policing, and it is even more difficult to state precisely what police agencies are doing with regard to it. The diversity of police programs that fit under the community policing umbrella has continued to increase. Community policing efforts involve the use of ombudsmen, coordinating councils, mobile and stationary ministations, victim services, organizational value and philosophy statements, enforcement crackdowns, advertising campaigns, problem-solving efforts, and foot, bike and horse patrols. This range of activities speaks well for the flexibility of the concept, but it demonstrates how difficult it is to define the practice of community policing or, more importantly, to evaluate its effectiveness. In 1988, Bayley expressed concern about this diversity:

> Despite the benefits claimed for community policing, programmatic implementation of it has been very uneven. Although widely, almost universally, said to be important, it means different things to different people—public relations campaigns, shopfront and mini-police stations, rescaled patrol beats, liaison with ethnic groups, permission for rank-and-file to speak to the press, Neighborhood Watch, foot patrols, patrol-detective teams, and door-to-door visits by police officers. Community policing on the ground often seems less a program than a set of aspirations wrapped in a slogan (p. 225).

Importantly, the issue became no clearer to Bayley as the years unfolded:

> Community policing means too many things to different people. Its practices are so varied that any evaluation will be partial or challengeable as not being authentic "community policing." Furthermore, because the mix of practices is so great, any evaluation will be *sui generis*, making generalization to other situations problematic (1994: 279).

The ambiguity of the concept and the apparent diversity of practices under the community policing umbrella have been challenged by Manning (1988), Greene and Mastrofski (1988) and Klockars (1988). These authors question whether community policing can result in substantive changes in police performance. Moore (1992) notes that "no police organizations in the United States have successfully made this change, [providing] powerful evidence of how hard it is" (p. 148). But Moore (1994) perceives the ambiguity of community policing as an asset:

> It is partly the ambiguity of the concept that is stimulating the wide pattern of experimentation we are observing. In this sense, it is important that the concept mean something, but not something too specific. The ambiguity is a virtue (p. 290).

Though the diversity of community policing efforts seems to defy simple definition, there have been a few attempts to offer an all-encompassing one. For example, Trojanowicz and Bucqueroux (1990) stated:

> Community policing is a new philosophy of policing, based on the concept that police officers and private citizens working together in creative ways can help solve contemporary community problems related to crime, fear of crime, social and physical disorder, and neighborhood decay (p. 5).

The Community Policing Consortium, a national coalition of four police organizations, defines community policing broadly as consisting of two basic components: problem solving and community engagement (Bureau of Justice Assistance 1994).

Rather than concretely define community policing, writers more often describe it by enumerating features commonly found in community policing programs. Skolnick and Bayley (1986: 211–220) describe four elements of community policing: police-community reciprocity, areal decentralization of command, reorientation of patrol toward more preventive tactics, and civilianization. Similarly, Goldstein (1987) lists four elements that are normally found in community policing:

> Most common among these are the involvement of the community in getting the police job done; the permanent assignment of police officers to a neighborhood in order to cultivate better relationships; the setting of police priorities based on the specific needs and desires of the community; and the meeting of these needs by the allocation of police resources and personnel otherwise assigned to responding to calls for police assistance (p. 7).

Bayley (1994) lists four elements: police consultation with communities, adaptation of police resources to local needs, mobilization of public and private resources, and addressing specific community problems by remedying the conditions that give rise to crime.

Constructing a definition of community policing would either be so broad as to include many traditional policing operations and tactics (e.g., a Police Athletic League or a crackdown on panhandlers after complaints from local merchants), or be so narrow as to exclude programs that could arguably be included in the definition. It must be agreed that there is no single operational definition of community policing. The broad definitional statements found in the theoretical literature on the subject are based on a limited number of departments' experience (usually one or two, and seldom more than five) or are prescriptive of what the author would like to see in policing. Though such definitions have value to police practitioners considering the implementation of community policing, it is unlikely that they reflect most agencies' actual experiences once implementation is under way.

Despite definitional limitations, there are some common perspectives and models found in descriptions of community policing programs. A review of these perspectives helps reveal some of the issues that emerge in studies of community policing.

PERSPECTIVES ON COMMUNITY POLICING

The literature on community policing suggests five perspectives on it. Though it is helpful to differentiate these perspectives to explore various meanings of community policing, the proponents of different perspectives often base their recommendations on the same evidence, and there is some overlap among the perspectives.

First, there is the deployment perspective on community policing. This is best exemplified in the early foot patrol studies (Trojanowicz n.d.; Police Foundation 1981). Here the focus is on placing officers in closer physical proximity to community members, especially in dense inner-city, high-crime neighborhoods. By getting out of their cars and detaching themselves from the dispatch system, officers can learn more about local concerns, distinguish between offenders and law-abiding residents, and prevent crime and disorder. While foot patrol and ministations are exemplars of this approach, beat profiling efforts (Boydston and Sherry 1975) and other schemes that emphasize tactics and procedures to improve officer knowledge of their territory and bring them into closer contact with citizens can be considered variations on the deployment perspective. New York's CPOP program—combining foot patrols and community profiling—incorporates the deployment perspective in its design (McElroy et al. 1989). Evaluations of foot patrol projects suggest they can be effective at reducing reported crime (Trojanowicz n.d.) and fear of crime (Police Foundation 1981). Unfortunately, these findings are not conclusive. The Police Foundation study of Newark, N.J., foot patrols concluded that crime was not reduced, thus placing it at odds with the conclusions of Trojanowicz. Also contradicting the Flint, Mich., findings, Bowers and Hirsch (1987) report that Boston's foot patrol project had no impact on crime or disorder. Pate (1989) reports that Baltimore's foot patrol experiment did not decrease victimization, fear of crime or disorder, though it did reduce reported crime. Thus, the Baltimore study contradicts the Newark findings but supports the Flint findings.

The community revitalization perspective articulated by Wilson and Kelling (1982, 1989) focuses on preventing the deterioration of neighborhoods by having the police pay closer attention to fear-inducing neighborhood characteristics. Unlike the deployment perspective, the community revitalization perspective focuses on the goals of policing. Considerable attention has been paid to this perspective in the academic literature. Studies by the Police Foundation in Houston and Newark provide mixed support for this perspective (Pate et al. 1986). Greene and Taylor (1988) critique this perspective and find little evidence to support its major hypotheses. Skogan (1990), on the other hand, finds support for the sequence of disorder, fear of crime, disinvestment in community, and criminal victimization. But Skogan's evidence raises questions about whether community policing can do much to interrupt this process. Others have attacked some of Wilson and Kelling's (1982) earlier proposals that suggest extralegal interventions to control disorder (Manning 1984; Klockars 1985).

The third approach to community policing can be found in Goldstein's problem perspective (1979, 1990). Goldstein focuses on the unit of police work and defines it as handling problems. The police, he contends, have become so immersed in administrative and management concerns that they fail to attend to the reasons police forces exist.

4

The goal of policing is to address the vast variety of problems of concern to citizens. Focusing on problems requires closer police-community relationships, because the police cannot effectively handle problems unless community members, other government agencies and private businesses participate in addressing these issues. How police are deployed is not a central concern in problem-oriented policing; the choice of using foot officers or officers on foot is less critical than the problem-solving efforts in which they engage. Community involvement in addressing problems may be one part of finding solutions, but many police problems are not area-specific, such as fear of crime, disorder or neighborhood deterioration. Domestic violence is an example of a serious problem that is generally unrelated to the notion of community as defined by geography. Instead, such a problem may more accurately involve a community of interest. Examples of a problem-oriented approach to policing are found in Baltimore County (Taft 1986; Cordner 1988), Newport News (Eck and Spelman 1987), San Diego, and Tulsa, Okla. (Weisel 1990). There are fewer evaluations of this perspective of community policing. Cordner (1986, 1988) evaluated the Baltimore County COPE unit's problem-solving efforts and found they were able to reduce crime and fear of crime as a result of most of those efforts. Eck and Spelman (1987) report that crime decreased due to three problem-solving efforts in Newport News. Capowich and Roehl (1994) found mixed results of problem solving in San Diego.

A fourth view of community policing is the customer perspective. Aspects of this approach can be found in the Madison, Wis., Police Department (Couper 1991; Wycoff and Skogan 1994) and Reno Police Department (Bradshaw 1990). This perspective focuses on developing proactive mechanisms—such as routine citizen surveys and citizen advisory groups—for determining the needs of the public relative to the police function. Like the deployment perspective, the customer perspective draws attention to procedures for "listening" to the public. Unlike the community revitalization and problem perspectives, it does not deal directly with the goals of policing. Perhaps for this reason, both Couper (1991) and Bradshaw (1990) also take a problem perspective.

The fifth perspective on community policing is the legitimacy perspective. Unlike the other perspectives, this perspective has no explicit advocates, though it may have much deeper roots in police history than any of the other perspectives. From a legitimacy perspective, community policing is an attempt by the police to be equitable and to be seen as equitable. This perspective draws attention to the fact that minority group members, particularly racial minorities, have historically been subject to more law enforcement activities than members of majority groups. Commonly cited evidence of this disparity is the disproportionate number of blacks and Hispanics arrested or shot by the police. Starting from this perspective, community policing opens a dialogue between the police and minority communities to address minority group concerns regarding police actions. Manifestations of a legitimacy perspective include regular meetings between high-level police commanders (including the chief or sheriff) and members of established minority group organizations. To the extent that the police department focuses most of its attention on officer sensitivity toward minority group members, the department is taking a legitimacy perspective to community policing. Some critics of community policing suggest that this approach is more window dressing than substance, that the police are trying to put themselves in a good light and placate dissatisfied citizens without making fundamental changes (see, for example, Klockars 1988).

As noted above, these five perspectives on community policing are seldom, if ever, found in their pure form within police agencies. Instead, departments mix these perspectives to varying degrees. San Diego provides an interesting example of how this mixing takes place. San Diego used a combination of the deployment and legitimacy perspectives in the mid-1970s. In 1988, the agency began applying the problem perspective along with the earlier perspectives. Similarly, the New York City Police Department's strategic plan for community policing (Brown 1991) describes components that draw variously on the deployment, revitalization, problem, and legitimacy perspectives.

MODELS OF COMMUNITY POLICING

There are other ways of looking at the range of approaches to community policing. Eck and Rosenbaum (1994) suggest three models that may underlie police departments' participation in community policing efforts. These models relate to three objectives: improving the efficiency of delivery of police services, achieving equitable delivery of services to all communities, and enhancing the effectiveness of police work (see Eck and Rosenbaum 1994, for further discussion of these models). As with the perspectives discussed in the previous section, community policing models are unlikely to be found in an organic state. Instead, most agencies link these models or shift organizational emphasis at different times.

The efficiency-based model of community policing tends to organize around changes in modes of policing, such as deployment methods, decentralization, telephone or walk-in reporting, foot patrol, and permanent beats. Models that relate to efficiency use a different approach to police work to make the best use of scarce resources. This model is most common where 911 calls are perceived as excessively burdensome and where financial resources for police personnel are in short supply. Addressing substantive community problems occurs within the background of the efficiency model.

The equity-based model of community policing, perhaps the most common model, often evolves based on demands for racial access and equity within a city. Such demands might include more personnel resources or greater access to police services. This model typically uses similar delivery mechanisms, such as community meetings, foot patrols, ministations or storefronts, walk-and-talk programs, or mounted patrol. For the most part, it is the form of police service delivery—designed to build trust between citizens and police or to "empower" citizens—rather than the substance of delivery that is the focus of equity-based models. Addressing substantive problems may be part of the approach, but it is usually secondary.

The effectiveness-based model of community policing represents a focus on substantive community problems. Although this model may use community-outreach approaches such as foot patrol or community meetings, the objective is to resolve substantive community problems. Community involvement is only a mechanism for doing so. Thus, this model normally involves identifying relevant stakeholders for specific problems, and these stakeholders vary from one problem to another. The effectiveness model seems to be more common where concerns regarding rapidly escalating crime and racial equity do not dominate the political agenda.

RESEARCH FINDINGS: FORM FOLLOWS FUNCTION

The five perspectives and three models discussed above all relate to a police agency's *motivations* for adopting community-oriented approaches to policing. The selection and implementation of any of these approaches or models to community policing thus depend on the objectives and motivations of those who have the vision or who are tasked with implementing community policing. Thus, community policing may be considered a means to an end. The desired end product may be improved relations with the minority community (the legitimacy perspective or equity model), and community policing may be a vehicle for achieving this objective. Similarly, a department overloaded with emergency calls may develop a method for prioritizing calls for service and open substations to facilitate citizen reporting. This approach reflects the efficiency model and the deployment and customer perspectives.

The goals or motivations for community policing suggest variation in the form of community policing adopted and the mechanisms for implementation. Objectives related to improving efficiency of police service, for example, are likely to reflect long-lasting mechanisms and changes in how police business is conducted. If an agency adopts the efficiency model, for example, and establishes a nonsworn community service officer component, such a program would be difficult to dismantle. Changes in deployment of current personnel—such as reassigning patrol officers to foot patrol teams—may relate to equity issues. Such an approach could be easily dismantled if other organizational priorities developed. Adopting the problem perspective and using the effectiveness model suggest a long-term organizational commitment requiring extensive training and permanent changes in organizational procedures such as performance evaluation and other techniques.

The community policing case studies PERF conducted revealed several key issues about the nature of community policing. Each case study discusses the activities in which police departments participate that are related to community policing. It should be noted that the community policing perspectives and models discussed previously were not considered during the site selection and data collection process. Through analysis of cases and cross-site comparisons of qualitative data, the research teams identified variation in motivation and objectives and their contribution to shaping an agency's community policing initiative as the primary research findings. Perhaps the most important questions asked during on-site data collection were the following:

> *Why* [emphasis added] did the department make the decision to develop a community policing program? How was the decision made? What historical events preceded the decision to implement community policing? Was there a key event that led to community policing being implemented?

The varying answers to this question seem to have played a major role in shaping the form of community policing each of the six agencies adopted. This chain of events will be apparent to the reader in the case studies, which constitute the rest of this report. For the agencies in this study, the answers related to the presence of a stimulus that motivated them to launch their community policing efforts. The research team was able to identify two primary stimuli that motivated movement toward community policing: troubled race relations, particularly between police and minority communities; and rising crime problems and difficulty in handling workload demands. A third motivation, difficult to classify as a stimulus, was the presence of police leaders with an articulated vision of what policing should be. The presence of such leaders occasionally constituted a stimulus, as when a new police chief took office. These varying motivations were not always clearly defined by the agency, but they were intuited through the data collection period. The first two of these stimuli suggest community policing emerged as a reaction to a condition; the latter stimulus reflected a proactive view of police work. One could deduce that police leaders of vision had yet to encounter problems of racial conflict and major crime, allowing them to take the high road. Such a conclusion, however, is beyond the scope of this research.

Importantly, each of the cases in this study reflects the importance of police leaders who pushed (or pulled) their agency toward community policing. While such leadership sometimes occurred at the level of chief, mid-ranking managers often played a key role in the process. This leadership effort generally reflected what is known as a change agent. Although the researchers made no particular effort to identify these change agents within organizations, their identity was readily apparent in most agencies. The absence of an identifiable change agent generally made the concept of community policing within an agency more difficult for police personnel to articulate.

The police departments in this study used a wide variety of organizational configurations to carry out community policing. Savannah and Newport News primarily used generalist patrol officers, supplemented, respectively, by bike and foot patrols and community stations; Las Vegas used a special-unit approach, a tactical team of officers; Santa Barbara effectively combined a special unit of problem-solving officers (known as beat coordinators) with a generalist approach in which patrol officers also participated in addressing problems; and Edmonton primarily used emergency response teams and decentralized community policing stations to handle citizens' problems. Philadelphia's approach to community policing seemed to be focused primarily at the captain level, with participation in community meetings and public outreach.

Organizational configurations to implement community policing also seemed to vary based on the type of model being implemented. For example, equity-based models seem more likely to use special units of personnel to interact with citizens. Effectiveness-based models are more likely to involve departmentwide participation in the community policing effort. Efficiency-based models may involve organizational changes but will not typically involve establishment of special units. These variations suggest that, in community policing efforts, form follows function.

The differing approaches to community policing can be categorized within the perspectives and models described previously. Santa Barbara, Savannah and Newport News use the problem perspective and the effectiveness model. Philadelphia and Las Vegas seem to reflect the legitimacy perspective and the equity model. Edmonton combines the efficiency and effectiveness models, reflecting the deployment and problem perspectives. The classification of agencies into these models suggests that each agency sought to achieve different goals, although in many cases, the research team deduced objectives that the departments never clearly stated. The absence of clearly stated goals was also apparent because of widespread confusion among officers about the nature and objectives of community policing within their own agency. Despite extensive training in some agencies, the research revealed that confusion—about goals, organizational direction and the meaning of community policing—was extremely common among police personnel. This finding suggests that extensive use of community policing rhetoric in agencies implementing community policing may be an important means of police leadership rather than the empty sloganeering-label linked with community policing rhetoric.

Confusion about departmental goals for community policing existed despite numerous organizational changes implemented to enhance it. Such changes involved departments' hiring and promotional practices, in-service training, establishment of fixed beats or steady shifts, modification of performance appraisals, establishment of internal communication practices, and so forth. Confusion among officers was minimized in agencies that invested more resources in communicating with them. Including community policing literature on promotional reading lists, providing extensive training and maintaining extensive interdepartmental communications helped to minimize confusion, and several departments had invested vast resources in such efforts. This investment of resources seemed to be necessary to permeate officers' traditional view of police work. The difficulty of this task may have been exacerbated by a tendency to view community policing as a fad that would change with the political winds of the various cities.

CONCLUSION

Police departments and cities implement community policing for radically different reasons. This variation in motivation or purpose results in differing forms of community policing by city and affects how community policing diffuses within different police departments.

The variation in community policing suggests that the concept makes sense only within the local context. Thus, the only appropriate method by which to evaluate community policing is not to contrast one police agency with another, but rather, to look within a *single* police agency to determine changes over time. Such changes may pertain to characteristics the department has sought to change. Of course, this suggests the agency's leadership must clearly state that agency's community policing objectives.

The variation in community policing approaches revealed in these six case studies suggests that further research can be done to assist with evaluating the effectiveness of alternative approaches. Although one could evaluate variations in police organizational approaches (e.g., the deployment perspective and efficiency model), there is nothing particularly new in the arena of alternative call-handling, decentralization efforts and deployment alternatives. More research and evaluation could be done on how police handle specific problems, particularly those that the community finds especially troubling, such as violent crime in specific neighborhoods, strong-arm robberies, youth-involved homicides, or other individual concerns (reflecting the problem perspective or effectiveness model). Little is known about these specific problems.

Further evaluation could reflect the success with which various police agencies achieve their objectives within their local context, such as improving perceptions regarding minority access to police services, reducing specific community problems or more efficiently managing departmental resources.

REFERENCES

Bayley, David H. (1988). "Community Policing: A Report From the Devil's Advocate," in Jack R. Greene and Stephen D. Mastrofski, eds., *Community Policing: Rhetoric or Reality.* New York: Praeger.

————. (1994). "International Differences in Community Policing," in Dennis P. Rosenbaum, ed., *The Challenge of Community Policing: Testing the Promises.* Thousand Oaks, Calif.: Sage Publications.

Bowers, William J., and Jon H. Hirsch (1987). "The Impact of Foot Patrol Staffing on Crime and Disorder in Boston: An Unmet Promise," *American Journal of Police* 6:17–44.

Boydston, John E., and Michael E. Sherry (1975). *San Diego Community Profile: Final Report.* Washington, D.C.: Police Foundation.

Bradshaw, R.V. (ed.) (1990). *Reno Police Department's Community-Oriented Policing—Plus.* Reno, Nev.: Reno Police Department.

Brown, Lee P. (1985). "Community-Policing Power Sharing," in William A. Geller, ed., *Police Leadership in America: Crisis and Opportunity.* New York: Praeger.

————. (1989). *Community Policing: A Practical Guide for Police Officials. Perspectives in Policing,* No. 12. Washington, D.C.: National Institute of Justice.

————. (1991). *Policing New York City in the 1990s: The Strategy for Community Policing.* New York: New York City Police Department.

Bureau of Justice Assistance (1994). *Understanding Community Policing: A Framework for Action.* Washington, D.C.: Community Policing Consortium.

Capowich, George E., and Janice E. Roehl (1994). "Problem-Oriented Policing: Actions and Effectiveness in San Diego," in Dennis P. Rosenbaum, ed., *The Challenge of Community Policing: Testing the Promises.* Thousand Oaks, Calif.: Sage Publications.

Cordner, Gary W. (1986). "Fear of Crime and the Police: An Evaluation of a Fear-Reduction Strategy," *Journal of Police Science and Administration* 14:223–233.

————. (1988). "A Problem-Oriented Approach to Community-Oriented Policing," in Jack R. Greene and Stephen D. Mastrofski, eds., *Community Policing: Rhetoric or Reality.* New York: Praeger.

Couper, David C., and Sabine H. Lobitz (1991). *Quality Policing: The Madison Experience.* Washington, D.C.: Police Executive Research Forum.

Eck, John E., and Dennis P. Rosenbaum (1994). "The New Police Order: Effectiveness, Equity and Efficiency in Community Policing," in Dennis P. Rosenbaum, ed., *The Challenge of Community Policing: Testing the Promises.* Thousand Oaks, Calif.: Sage Publications.

Goldstein, Herman (1979). "Improving Policing: A Problem-Oriented Approach," *Crime and Delinquency* 25:236–258.

————. (1987). "Toward Community-Oriented Policing: Potential, Basic Requirements and Threshold Questions," *Crime and Delinquency* 33:6–30.

————. (1990). *Problem-Oriented Policing.* New York: McGraw-Hill.

Greene, Jack R., and Stephen D. Mastrofski (eds.) (1988). *Community Policing: Rhetoric or Reality.* New York: Praeger.

Klockars, Carl B. (1985). "Order Maintenance, the Quality of Urban Life and Police: A Different Line of Argument," in William A. Geller, ed., *Police Leadership in America: Crisis and Opportunity.* New York: Praeger.

———. (1988). "The Rhetoric of Community Policing," in Jack R. Greene and Stephen D. Mastrofski, eds., *Community Policing: Rhetoric or Reality*. New York: Praeger.

Manning, Peter K. (1984). "Community Policing," *American Journal of Police* 3:205–227.

———. (1988). "Community Policing as a Drama of Control," in Jack R. Greene and Stephen D. Mastrofski, eds., *Community Policing: Rhetoric or Reality*. New York: Praeger.

Mastrofski, Stephen D. (1988). "Community Policing as Reform: A Cautionary Tale," in Jack R. Greene and Stephen D. Mastrofski, eds., *Community Policing: Rhetoric or Reality*. New York: Praeger.

McElroy, Jerome E., Colleen A. Cosgrove, and Susan Sadd (1989). "An Examination of the Community Patrol Officer Program (CPOP) in New York City." Unpublished report. New York: Vera Institute of Justice.

Moore, Mark H. (1992). "Community Policing," in Michael Tonry and Norval Morris, eds., *Modern Policing*. Chicago: University of Chicago Press.

Murphy, Chris, and Graham Muir (1985). *Community-Based Policing: A Review of the Critical Issues*. Ottawa, Ontario: Solicitor General of Canada.

Pate, Antony M. (1989). "Community-Oriented Policing in Baltimore," in Dennis Jay Kenney, ed., *Police and Policing: Contemporary Issues*. New York: Praeger.

Pate, Antony M., Mary Ann Wycoff, Wesley G. Skogan, and Lawrence W. Sherman (1986). *Reducing Fear of Crime in Houston and Newark: A Summary Report*. Washington, D.C.: Police Foundation.

Police Foundation (1981). *The Newark Foot Patrol Experiment*. Washington, D.C.: Police Foundation.

Rosenbaum, Dennis P. (ed.) (1994). *The Challenge of Community Policing: Testing the Promises*. Thousand Oaks, Calif.: Sage Publications.

Skogan, Wesley G. (1990). *Disorder and Decline: Crime and Decline: Crime and the Spiral of Decay in American Neighborhoods*. New York: Free Press.

Skolnick, Jerome H., and David H. Bayley (1986). *The New Blue Line: Police Innovations in Six American Cities*. New York: Free Press.

Sparrow, Malcolm K., Mark H. Moore, and David M. Kennedy (1990). *Beyond 911: A New Era for Policing*. New York: Basic Books.

Taft, Philip B., Jr. (1986). *Fighting Fear: The Baltimore County C.O.P.E. Project*. Washington, D.C.: Police Executive Research Forum.

Toch, Hans, and J. Douglas Grant (1991). *Police as Problem Solvers*. New York: Plenum.

Trojanowicz, Robert C. (n.d.). *An Evaluation of the Neighborhood Foot Patrol Program in Flint, Michigan*. East Lansing, Mich.: Neighborhood Foot Patrol Center, Michigan State University.

Trojanowicz, Robert C., and Bonnie Bucqueroux (1989). *Community Policing: A Contemporary Perspective*. Cincinnati: Anderson.

Wadman, Robert C., and Robert K. Olson (1990). *Community Wellness: A New Theory of Policing*. Washington, D.C.: Police Executive Research Forum.

Weatheritt, Mollie (1988). "Community Policing: Rhetoric or Reality," in Jack R. Greene and Stephen D. Mastrofski, eds., *Community Policing: Rhetoric or Reality.* New York: Praeger.

Weisel, Deborah Lamm (1990). "Playing the Home Field: A Problem-Oriented Approach to Drug Control," *American Journal of Police* 9:75–95.

Wilson, James Q., and George L. Kelling (1982). "Broken Windows: The Police and Neighborhood Safety," *The Atlantic Monthly* (March):29–38.

———— (1989). "Making Neighborhoods Safe," *The Atlantic Monthly* (February):46–52.

Wycoff, Mary Ann, and Wesley G. Skogan (1994). "Community Policing: An Analysis of Implementation and Impact," in Dennis P. Rosenbaum, ed., *The Challenge of Community Policing: Testing the Promises.* Thousand Oaks, Calif.: Sage Publications.

Ready, Fire, Aim:[1]
A Look at Community Policing in Edmonton, Alberta, Canada

by Carl W. Hawkins Jr.

INTRODUCTION

Downtown Edmonton business owners and office workers were complaining to Constable[2] Patricia Murray about the panhandlers in the area. According to Murray, "The complaints included that these people smelled bad, asked for money and were alcoholic or drug dependent." The business owners and office workers wanted the police to do something.

Murray looked into the problem. She found that the panhandlers were concentrated in five areas, and based on her research, she concluded there were three viable courses of action the police department could take. One option was to arrest the panhandlers, another was to move them out by any means, and the third was to have the business owners create a paper voucher system for basic necessities. She knew the first two options had been tried in many cities, with limited success. "The problem was one of perception; most citizens wanted to help the panhandlers by giving them money," she said. This only escalated the problem, she concluded, by drawing even more panhandlers to the area. Murray recommended that a paper voucher system be established.

The system allowed downtown business owners to print paper vouchers that they then sold to customers. These vouchers could be redeemed only for food, nonalcoholic drinks or bus transportation. The panhandlers received the paper vouchers from citizens who would normally have given them money. Murray said, "A lot of education had to be done to have the public use the voucher system," but she believed this approach would reduce the problem.

This is an example of community policing in Edmonton in 1993. It had not always been that way; historically, the department policed the city in a more traditional way. A quick look back shows how community policing has evolved in Edmonton from its traditional roots.

THE HISTORY OF EDMONTON, ALBERTA, CANADA

The capital of Alberta, Canada, Edmonton owes its existence to an abundant supply of natural resources. These resources prompted each of its three major growth periods. In 1795, the Hudson Bay Company founded Fort Edmonton on the banks of the North Saskatchewan River. Traders bartered with native Indians for mink and fox pelts. A trading settlement developed and became the main stopping point for routes to the north and west.

---

1. This case study's title is taken from chapter 8 of *In Search of Excellence,* by Thomas J. Peters and Robert H. Waterman Jr.

2. A constable is the equivalent of an American police officer.

During the 1800s, Edmonton also became a starting point for gold prospectors rushing to the Klondike region. Gold diggers stocked up on supplies in Edmonton for the harsh trip north. When the gold failed to materialize for some, they headed back to Edmonton to settle for a slower but surer way of life. The city grew to six times its previous size, making it a prime choice for the provincial capital when Alberta was formed in 1905.

In the years that followed, Edmonton earned the nickname "Gateway to the North" because of its status as a transportation hub and gateway to regions beyond. In 1915, the city became a major link to the Canadian Pacific Transcontinental Railroad and emerged as an important crossroads for travel.

Edmonton's reputation as a gateway city was reinforced during the 1930s, when pilots transported vital medical supplies, food and mail to the north. When construction began on the Alaska Highway in 1942, the city again found itself in the role of major transportation and supply center.

Just as the last big growth period was fading from memory, the Leduc Number One Well, approximately 25 miles southeast of Edmonton, gushed forth black crude oil in 1947. This was just the beginning. Since then, more than 2,250 wells have been drilled around the city. Enormous industrial growth resulted, and the city's population quadrupled. Today, over 600,000 people live in Edmonton.

THE HISTORY OF LAW ENFORCEMENT IN EDMONTON

In the early 1870s, the new Dominion government established law enforcement in Edmonton by providing it a contingent of officers known as the North West Mounted Police. As a result of "stirred up political trouble" in 1892 between this agency and the Edmonton City Council, the city began hiring a group of officers who later became the Edmonton City Police. Although the origins of the Edmonton City Police were rooted in the conflict between the city council and the mounted police, the agency's early history was shaped by chief constables who came from the Royal Canadian Mounted Police (RCMP).

In the early 1900s, the police focused primarily on liquor violations, prostitution and gambling. Several chief constables were fired for not addressing these problems. During World War I, Edmonton police leaders placed an extreme emphasis on discipline and the use of the military model for command and control. In the 1930s and 1940s, the advent of the automobile, radio communications and other developing technologies moved the Edmonton City Police into a new era of policing.

On Sept. 27, 1954, the Edmonton City Council chose M.F.E. Anthony, who had worked as an assistant RCMP commissioner, as the new chief constable. Anthony instituted many changes in the city police, including the establishment of new sections or units such as central registry, case supervisors, crime index, communications, garage, drawing office, and personnel. For greater efficiency, existing divisions were broken down into smaller squads. The first-ever recruit training class graduated in 1955. Also during Anthony's tenure, the police moved into newly renovated police headquarters. During this period, Edmonton annexed several surrounding towns, and the city population began to rise again.

In the mid-1960s, the city council created and appointed the Edmonton Board of Police Commissioners. This board was formed to serve as a buffer between the city government, the police department and the public. Shortly thereafter, Anthony died and was succeeded by two other chief constables who had also worked for the RCMP.

READY: THE LUNNEY YEARS

In 1974, the city council appointed yet another RCMP member, Robert F. Lunney, to head the Edmonton City Police. Lunney, who had been the superintendent in charge of classification and compensation, had received two national awards for his contributions to policing prior to his appointment. These awards and Lunney's high ethical standards brought a new sense of pride and professionalism to the office. Staff Sgt.[3] Keith "P.J." Duggan reflected, "Prior to Bob Lunney becoming chief, officers were hired by the pound [i.e., the bigger, the better], and the police were seen as [engaged] in a war."

Lunney also brought to the department a general concern for the constables and a sense of openness. "Lunney would walk around the department and know each officer's name, spouse's name and children's names," added Duggan. Once, Lunney walked into a parade (roll call) and noticed that the cross straps over the constables' handguns could easily come off, which could be dangerous. The constables had been concerned about this for some time. Lunney asked whether the cross straps were necessary, and when shown how easily they came off, he ordered that their use be discontinued. Duggan stated, "Lunney, by that one act, demonstrated his concern for the constable on the street."

During Lunney's tenure, another growth period for Edmonton was under way, due to an oil boom. As the population rapidly grew, so did the police department. Recruit training classes graduated every 15 weeks, one after another. The average amount of police experience per officer declined from 13 years to 18 months, according to Duggan. Also, Edmonton was attracting single males "without high life skills" from all over North America to work in the oil fields. The period from the late 1970s to the early 1980s was one of the most unstable times for the police department, but it also provided an opportunity for Lunney to change the department's culture.

Monthly meetings were held at which the constables could provide input about issues facing the department. Safety, job functions, weapons, holsters, uniforms, and beards were discussed at these meetings. Other changes were implemented: school resource officers were stationed in schools; the victim services, street crimes and child abuse units were established; and community service officer positions were created. The departmental changes reflected a sense of social consciousness regarding the policing of Edmonton. The agency's name was changed from the Edmonton City Police to the Edmonton Police Department, and the title of chief constable was changed to chief of police.

In 1984, Lunney approved a sabbatical for Inspector Chris Braiden, so he could work for the Solicitor General's Office in Ottawa, Canada. During his tenure as a special advisor to the solicitor general on policing, Braiden focused his efforts on reading, traveling and collecting information that sharpened his views of community policing and problem solving. Braiden found support compatible with his view of how police services should be delivered. The experience also gave him ideas, knowledge and access to people who would be helpful to him later in further refining his vision of community policing. The seeds of change—young officers, openness, a new chief, community consciousness, research on community policing—were planted during Lunney's tenure. The Edmonton Police Department became "used to change" and was poised and ready for a new style of policing.

FIRE: NEIGHBORHOOD FOOT PATROL

During the 1980s, the Edmonton oil boom began to slow down. For economic reasons, the police department stopped hiring new constables; in fact, there was a call to start laying off constables. In 1983, the entire department elected not to accept a pay raise to preserve 86 constables' jobs.

---

3. A staff sergeant is the equivalent of an American lieutenant.

Braiden returned from his sabbatical and was promoted to superintendent in 1987. Upon his return, Braiden was full of new ideas for policing and insisted that the Edmonton Police Department look into community-based approaches to policing. However, Lunney was not in a position to make such a decision, as he was planning to retire soon from the department.

The selection of a new police chief provided Braiden with a unique opportunity. He applied for the position so he could argue his case for neighborhood foot patrols before the police commission. Commission members asked Braiden many questions about community policing during his interview, but they ultimately appointed Leroy Chahley to be the new chief. Chahley was concerned with managing internal departmental problems; he did not become active in the neighborhood foot patrol movement.

In April 1987, Chahley agreed to let neighborhood foot patrols be implemented in 21 of Edmonton's most problematic areas. Braiden sought out and obtained additional monies from Canada's solicitor general and the Mott Foundation to help fund the program and pay for an evaluator. Twenty-one neighborhood foot patrol constables with 40 hours of training were assigned to the city's hottest areas, as identified through an examination of 153,000 calls for service. (Significantly, 81 percent of the calls in these areas were repeat calls.) Braiden issued beepers to the foot patrol constables and helped them set up neighborhood offices equipped with telephones and answering machines. The constables' objectives were to work with the community in solving problems and to decentralize operations by answering calls for service from their beat offices. Braiden told them, "I want people contact, not pavement contact." He added: "You must go to where the people are. If they are inside, you must go inside." As the problem areas changed, Braiden directed the neighborhood foot patrols to new problem areas.

One of the new foot patrol constables was Dave Hut. He found he was getting a high number of repeat calls regarding public drunkenness and general disturbances from a neighborhood near the downtown area. Traditionally, the Edmonton Police Department responded to this problem by arresting inebriated people and keeping them in jail until they sobered up. Hut studied the problem and discovered that the offenders' drink of choice was Chinese cooking wine. This substance was 38 percent alcohol, easy to obtain and very inexpensive. The wine's salt content was so high that ingesting it was sometimes fatal.

Hut contacted the Alberta Liquor Control Board and found that because the cooking wine contained so much salt, it was not classified as an alcoholic beverage and could not be regulated under the Liquor Control Act. The constable approached Canadian Customs and tried to limit importation of the wine. This tactic proved unsuccessful because the wine was not considered alcoholic, and therefore, it was not taxable or under Customs' control.

Hut organized a meeting with the police commission, Solicitor General's Office representatives, Liquor Control Board, and Edmonton Police Department members. The Liquor Control Board agreed to change its policy to include the cooking wine in its definition of alcoholic substances.

The wine could then be regulated under the Liquor Control Act, which prohibited the sale of any alcohol-based product that was over 20 percent alcohol per volume. Also, because the wine would be considered alcohol, it consequently would be subject to an importation tax. Eventually, the importation of the wine was banned under the Liquor Control Act. Although the area still had its share of alcoholics, they no longer succumbed to the effects of the deadly cooking wine.

Joe Hornick, executive director of the Canadian Research Institute for Law and the Family at the University of Calgary, evaluated the neighborhood foot patrol program and found that its objectives were met: repeat calls for service decreased, reporting of information to the police increased, community problems were solved, job satisfaction among constables increased, and citizens were more satisfied with the police. Hornick recommended that the program be expanded to other high-calls-for-service areas so other constables would have the autonomy to deal with problems in their communities.

AIM: LOOKING AT THE STRUCTURE WITHIN

Even with the success of the neighborhood foot patrol program, Chahley was preoccupied with the internal problems facing the Edmonton Police Department. Several constables were arrested for crimes, and the press began to pressure Chahley about the department's problems; at times, it seemed as though every day brought a new encounter with the press over internal problems. During this time, Chahley strengthened the department's unity of command and created platoons and squads.

In 1988, the department received accreditation through the Commission on Accreditation for Law Enforcement Agencies. Inspector Roger Simms, the accreditation manager, felt community policing and accreditation were mutually reinforcing. According to Simms, accreditation helped the police elicit community support and fostered interaction. "Many of the concepts of community policing are built into the standards," said Simms. For example, standard 54.2.10 required the police agency to seek input from the community so that the agency's policies would reflect the community's needs. Standard 45.2.3 required the agency to conduct drug-related crime prevention programs in schools, as well as conduct security surveys and encourage citizens to properly mark their property so it could be recovered if stolen. These and many other standards convinced Simms that accreditation provided the department with a foundation to address problems and community needs.

During this period, additional technology became available to the department. The identification section obtained an automated fingerprint and identification system, and mobile digital terminals were installed in police vehicles.

During the city's economic decline in the 1980s, the population increased significantly, which led to more calls for police service and more reported crime. Because of the city's economic difficulties, the Edmonton Police Department did not hire any additional constables during that decade. Even with these mounting concerns, the neighborhood foot patrol program continued to operate and brought some problems under control.

Constable Lew Evans-Davies patrolled a neighborhood with a large number of apartment buildings. The majority of the apartment residents received social assistance. Because the apartment mailboxes were located outside the security doors, anyone could access them. Thieves began stealing government checks from the mailboxes, frequently cashing them with phony identification. Evans-Davies felt new tactics were necessary to address this problem, as the traditional law enforcement approach was not working. Evans-Davies contacted the city newspaper, which published an article titled "Operation Bank It." This article led to a television story. The media coverage informed the public about the problem and introduced them to the concept of direct deposit.

The direct deposit program allowed the social service agency to electronically transfer a check into a recipient's bank account. Evans-Davies also circulated information pamphlets and questionnaires to the apartment residents to both educate them about the problem and elicit additional information about the thefts. The building managers cooperated by moving the mailboxes behind the security doors.

These tactics eliminated mailbox damage and check theft. The amount of money lost by the companies that cashed the checks was also reduced.

READY: A MANDATE FOR CHANGE

From 1980 to 1990, Edmonton's population increased by 19 percent, and reported crime increased by 44 percent. With the economic downturn creating budget shortfalls, the police department was faced with the prospect of having no new constables to handle the increase in calls for service. In 1991, the city council cut $1.7 million from the police department budget. As a result, the department was unable to hire additional constables for the ninth straight year, despite a population increase of 100,000 since 1983. Norm Koch, of the Edmonton Police Association, stated, "If the public [were] aware of how [few] officers there are out there, it would be alarmed." Inspector Hugh Richards added, "We're finding guys who joined in 1987 saying, 'I'm drained; I can't take any more of this.'" Adding to the stress was an angry public complaining about being kept waiting. Emergency calls still received a quick response, but other calls did not.

Koch told of a complaint that was held for seven hours because no constables were available to respond. "I'm not sure about neighborhood foot patrol walking up and down the street holding hands with businessmen. It's great policing within a three-block area, and the rest of the area gets only standard policing," he said.

Braiden continued speaking to various police groups, the community and the police commission about his vision of a new style of policing, which he called community-based policing. "Policing must get back to its roots—policing of the people, by the people, for the people," said Braiden, paraphrasing Abraham Lincoln and Sir Robert Peel. "I get exasperated when people say community-based policing is new. Who in the hell were the police ever intended to police but the community?" added Braiden. The former chair of the police commission, Zaheer Lakhani, said he heard Braiden speak about community-based policing several times. He added, "We also read many of the publications about this type of policing, and it made sense." Horner's evaluation also gave the police commission some assurance that the Edmonton Police Department was on the right track and that, perhaps, community-based policing was the answer to the city's crime and disorder problems.

In 1992, the new chair of the police commission, Wayne Drewry, stated that "Chris Braiden got us all revved up about community-based policing [as] being the way to police smarter." A variety of factors contributed to the police commission's decision that the Edmonton Police Department would embrace community-based policing. They included Edmonton's economic difficulties, Braiden's leadership, police commission members' exposure to community-based policing concepts, and public support for neighborhood foot patrol constables.

On New Year's Day, 1990, the name of the Edmonton Police Department was changed to the Edmonton Police Service. Chahley retired later that year, and the search was on for a new police chief. After many interviews, the police commission selected Doug McNally. A career officer who had risen through the ranks, McNally knew of the problems facing the city and the department. When he was hired, the police commission told him they wanted the city to practice community-based policing. McNally stated, "We must be careful and not use labels; we should police the way it was meant to be." He added, "We should empower the community to solve their own problems, while providing them with a better product." McNally also knew from his prior experience that to keep policing the city in the traditional way, he would need 200 new constables and $12 million in additional funding—and there was little chance the city council would give him either. Regardless, McNally knew changes had to be made.

McNally asked Braiden to take on the job of expanding community-based policing across one of four divisions. Braiden agreed, on two conditions: he wanted community-based policing to occur across the board, and he wanted to formulate a plan for making this happen. McNally agreed, and Braiden started working on a blueprint for change.

Braiden's blueprint was called "A Process for Change." In it, Braiden proposed five steps:

- an organizational review;

- an in-depth analysis of workload;

- a decentralization through the addition of neighborhood foot patrols, satellite police offices and wheeled trailers that could be used for problems of a transient nature;

- a reevaluation of specialization; and

- a stratification of the service delivery system around a four-tiered level of delivery: high-priority units, complaint units, satellite police offices, and neighborhood foot patrols.

Braiden next proposed a team retreat for the department's executive officers to "tell us where everybody stands and enable us to get a consensus on the core components of the overall project." Braiden also asked that all six superintendents be full-time members of the proposed project team. "Each must have a piece of the action so that they each have a vested interest in its success or failure," stated Braiden.

Braiden called for the establishment of a community-based policing project team to conduct an organizational review, and he looked for volunteers throughout the department. In May 1990, Braiden selected four members to serve on the team, based on their knowledge of departmental operations. Braiden told them there were two basic rules he wanted them to follow: "I would rather you ask for forgiveness than permission," and "Don't ask a question if you can live without the answer."

Within a few months, the executive officer's team retreat was held, and the process of change Braiden proposed was adopted. At the retreat, the team adopted the phrase "Committed to Community Needs" as the Edmonton Police Service's core value. They also vowed to implement community-based policing throughout the department.

In March 1991, the community-based policing project team conducted a complete organizational review of the Edmonton Police Service. They did so with an eye toward limiting specialization and centralization, as Braiden did not like either. He often said, "Generalize whenever possible, specialize when necessary, decentralize whenever possible, centralize when necessary." Braiden felt specialization and centralization added to the bureaucracy that hindered the agency's community-based policing efforts. "What happened to the Edmonton Police Service is what happens to all bureaucracies on the public dollar that have a monopoly on their product," he said. "Over time, the product becomes what those on the inside want it to be. The only way the police can get back to being a real part of the community they are charged with serving is by dismantling the bureaucratic structure that isolates them from the community." Braiden insisted that the Edmonton Police Service needed a "bureaucratic garage sale."

The organizational review achieved two things: it eliminated parts of the old system that were contrary to the department's new core value, and it freed up resources to build a new organization. The organizational review looked at the department from two perspectives: the "big picture," or a bird's-eye view of the agency, and the unit analysis, or a review of the details of the organization.

The "big picture" review documented that the department was in its 10th year of "cutback management" and employed 28 fewer constables than it had a decade before—despite the fact that the population had increased by 105,000 and that calls for service had increased proportionately over the same period. The unit analysis showed that, due to increased specialization, the number of organizational units increased from 64 to 120 between 1974 and 1988. The number of constables assigned to calls for service dropped from 545 to 468. As part of the analysis, review team members also visited each unit to determine its role within the organization and see whether its activities were aligned with its original purpose.

An 11-member evaluation team made up of department leaders from many sections and ranks examined the organizational review findings and made 164 recommendations. After five intense days of review, the group approved 132 of the recommendations for inclusion in the final recommendation package. As a result of this process, 68 department members were moved to front-end positions, which helped improve the response to community needs. Additional recommendations were delayed until approval of the 1992 budget.

In December 1991, the community-based policing project team concentrated on completing a workload analysis to determine how to redesign the districts and where to place new facilities. From this analysis, the team decided that some city areas needed closer attention than others. This in-depth analysis provided the rationale for new beat boundaries.

Also in December 1991, the project team started working on the department's new service delivery model. The model proposed the following:

- the opening of 12 community stations throughout the city where citizens could report nonemergency incidents in person,

- a "red page" insert in the telephone directory to encourage citizens to call or go to a community station for service,

- a new call path chart to enable complaint evaluators and station members to determine the most effective way to resolve calls for service,

- a first-contact reporting concept to reduce repetitive information-gathering,

- a mobile digital terminal reporting system to reduce paperwork and processing time, and

- a delayed response procedure for nonemergency incidents to allow for a later response at a mutually agreed-on time.

The new service delivery model was designed to divert as many reports as possible to community stations and, at the same time, to reduce the number of fraudulent reports by requiring citizens to report incidents in person. Detective David Veitch, who worked on developing the model, said the Edmonton Police Service predicted over 100,000 calls for service would be routed to community stations rather than to central police headquarters as a result of the changes.

The model also established a four-tiered response: priority 1 - immediate, priority 2 - urgent, priority 3 - service, and priority 4 - delayed. The model further established four types of constables for delivering police services: neighborhood foot patrol constables, ownership constables, community station constables, and response constables. Any constable in an area, regardless of type, would respond to priority 1 and priority 2 calls. Ownership and response constables would respond to priority 3 calls. Priority 4 calls that were not picked up voluntarily through call stopping would be assigned at parade (roll call) and monitored by area supervisors. Many of the priority 3 calls would end up being handled at the community stations. Also, many additional calls would go directly to the neighborhood foot patrol and ownership constables through their answering machines, beepers or cellular phones, thereby bypassing centralized police operations. This layered process was designed to increase face-to-face contacts and free constables to do more problem solving, while continuing to handle true emergencies.

The concept of constables' "ownership" of specific geographical areas was integrated into many of the design functions of community-based policing in Edmonton. "The only way to motivate anyone in the workplace is to give them meaningful work and control over that work," claimed Braiden, adding that "all attempts at external motivation have failed, whether they are better salaries, fringe benefits, less hours, human relations training, sensitivity training, or communications training." The establishment of ownership and neighborhood foot patrol constables was designed to give the constables meaningful work and control over that work.

One of the areas that was most affected by decentralization and despecialization in the department was the criminal investigations division. After the changes, most detectives worked out of district stations and reported to the station commanders. A few detectives, for the most part specialists in violent crime, worked out of headquarters. Criminal investigations division Superintendent Al Buerger said Edmonton detectives saw many benefits from community-based policing. He stated: "In the past, we had everybody to talk to and nobody to talk to. Now we know who works a geographic area and can pass information back and forth to the constables." He added that not all problems were geographically based, and therefore, detectives could see problems that occurred in other communities. This enabled detectives to solve problems they may have missed by concentrating on neighborhoods alone. Buerger claimed that decentralization and despecialization alone did nothing to change investigations work, because many communities do not have geographical boundaries, but rather, are spread throughout the city. Similar interests bring members of nongeographical communities, such as a city's business community, together. A centralized group of investigators can address their concerns more directly than a neighborhood constable or detective can.

During this time, detectives became involved in many problem-solving initiatives. Detective Ken Montgomery told of an Edmonton service station chain that was open 24 hours a day and accounted for 27 percent of all city robberies. Some of the robberies were internal. Montgomery stated: "One of the biggest problems was that the service stations had very little security. Cigarettes were out in the open for anyone to steal, most of the money was kept in the registers, and employees were not screened before they were hired." Montgomery went to the service stations and put basic crime prevention measures in place. He also set up a security check system under which any person whom the service stations were to hire had to be cleared by the Edmonton Police Service. He also asked the owner to contact him any time there was a robbery or theft at the stations. After these measures were instituted, the robbery rate at this chain dropped to levels comparable to those of other city service stations.

FIRE: COMMUNITY-BASED POLICING IN EDMONTON

On Jan. 6, 1992, at a special meeting of the Edmonton Board of Police Commissioners, McNally presented all the proposed changes relating to the implementation of community-based policing in the city. The police commission adopted the proposals.

The Edmonton Police Service began the implementation process with a media blitz informing citizens of how they could request police services at their community stations. Radio and television spots, as well as newspaper advertisements and articles regarding the new process, were run. The ads dramatized the old way Edmonton police provided services. They showed citizens waiting on the phone for a call-taker, and then waiting even longer for an officer to arrive. The ads also explained how convenient the community stations were to where citizens lived, and how easy it was to report complaints to uniformed constables at the stations. The telephone company provided a red, one-page directory insert that explained where to go to make nonemergency requests for service. All utility customers were sent a flier with a label they could place by their phone with directions on how to report nonemergency problems.

When opened, community stations were staffed 12 hours a day, every day except Sunday, on which they were open from 10 a.m. to 6 p.m. Uniformed constables and volunteers were available to assist the public. The stations were equipped with telephones, copiers, fax machines, mobile digital terminals, and other office equipment. The stations handled motor vehicle accidents in which the cars could be moved, vehicle thefts, general thefts, mischief and vandalism, lost and found property, minor assaults, and ongoing problems.

Within one month, the department's organizational studies unit began to evaluate the media campaign's impact. A random-sample survey of Edmonton residents revealed that

- over 97 percent knew there were community stations in their areas;

- 51 percent learned about the community stations from the media, with newspapers being the most frequently cited source of information; and

- before the media campaign, only 15 percent would likely go to their community stations for police services, but after the media campaign, 22 percent would.

The training of all employees in problem solving, community policing concepts and the new service delivery model began in October 1991. McNally spoke at most sessions and provided statistics demonstrating why community-based policing was necessary for the city. Braiden and Buerger delivered portions of the training, as well. The number of neighborhood foot patrol constables increased to 27, and the new ownership constables started working their assignments.

A new performance evaluation system was developed during this time. The performance evaluation covered aspects of community-based policing and problem solving. One section evaluated constables on their conflict resolution skills and proactive project work, as well as their efforts to target disorder, network with the private sector and interact with the public. Superintendent John LaFlamme stated, "We recognize success, with a tolerance for failure." LaFlamme added that the police service was working to develop constable I and II ranks to recognize officers with a minimum number of years of experience who passed the required promotional tests.

By the end of 1992, several results of the community-based policing effort were evident. According to Veitch, complaints and total calls decreased by about 30 percent, indicating that many calls were being handled at the community stations. "We've had 200,000 people walk into our community police stations in 1992 to report problems or ask for advice," added McNally. The number rose to 235,000 in 1993. Veitch also related that "abandoned calls" decreased by 36 percent, indicating that fewer people were hanging up after being put on hold, and that telephone calls for service were answered 40 percent quicker than before. Nonemergency calls that were dispatched were also handled quicker than before; there was almost a one-hour reduction in response time to these calls, according to Veitch.

But not everyone was so optimistic. One researcher was concerned that community-based policing in Edmonton might be in some trouble. The only department personnel who interacted with the community were the constables on the street and the executive officers. The middle managers interacted only with each other. The researcher believed a flattening of the organization was in order. He also felt that during tough economic times, the community-based policing plan might be streamlined. For example, in one area, neighborhood foot patrol offices were closed and constables were told to work out of the community stations.

Another area of concern was the ownership constables' role. Ownership Constable Jerry Vercammen stated, "I spend about 80 percent of my time on calls for service and about 20 percent of my time on problems in my ownership area." He felt the department should look at ways to better define the ownership constable's role and free up more time for addressing problems.

Some of the neighborhood foot patrol constables were concerned about the lack of training for this new assignment. When the first constables were assigned to the new program in 1988, they received 40 hours of training. Due to attrition over the next three years, new neighborhood foot patrol constables were assigned to the program, but many received no training. One neighborhood foot patrol constable said, "All I received in the way of training was that I walked with another constable for two days and was told to take ownership of the area."

AIM: THE FUTURE

McNally viewed further stratification of the constables' roles as one of the last steps to be taken to fully implement community-based policing in Edmonton. His plan included assigning new recruit graduates as response constables. As constables gained more experience and improved their job skills, they could progress from handling calls to working at community stations. With more experience and improvement, they could be assigned as ownership constables, and their last assignment would be as neighborhood foot patrol constables.

The Operational Support Communications and Records System was being developed to provide constables with the latest information on repeat calls in their neighborhoods. This system is designed to encode data on previous calls and dispositions and integrate this information into future calls for service. Mike Derbyshire, who was working on the system, said, "The system will provide information by geographic area, address or community league." According to Derbyshire, this should enable constables to have the latest information on problems in their areas.

In February 1993, Braiden retired from the Edmonton Police Service to devote more time to lecturing and sharing his vision of policing. He noted that some officers do not easily form the bonds with the public that are needed for a police-citizen partnership, which he believes is at the heart of community-based policing. "When the police work alone, without public help, they solve less than 10 percent of criminal cases. With a lead, a kick-start from somebody in the public, there is more than an 85 percent success rate," he estimated.

With Braiden's retirement, Inspector Hugh Richards took over the community-based policing project. Richards believed that the Edmonton Police Service was well on its way in the implementation process, and that there was no turning back. Other project team members concurred. Sgt. Tony Harder felt that the patrol force bought into the change the most, and that other divisions were moving in the same direction. Staff Sgt. P.J. Duggan agreed, adding, "Most change is generational." He thought the change would be complete once most of the old guard retired.

At the end of February 1993, all north division constables and supervisors met at a luncheon to discuss ownership. The issue of ownership was creating some problems in the stratification process, and the north division was trying to work through these concerns with input from everyone in the division. Many questions were asked at the meeting, and they continue to frame the evolution of community policing: Should the number of ownership constables be increased or decreased? Should the geographic areas be enlarged or reduced? Should the ownership constables be on day shift or be rotated through the shifts? The meeting also sparked many heated discussions between constables who were not convinced that there was much difference between the ownership and response constables, except for some flexibility. The ownership issue remains to be resolved, and experimentation continues. McNally stated: "There are no models out there. We are trying things, fixing them and making things work. When I leave this service, I want to go back and speak to the ownership constables. If they understand the concept of ownership, then we will have fully reached community-based policing in Edmonton."

Community Policing in Las Vegas:
Back to the Basics in a High-Stakes Town

by Mike Butler

INTRODUCTION

Life is simple and safe in a quiet little town called Mayberry. There, every friendly face is a familiar one to the two-man police force that protects the town. Strolling from the barbershop to the general store, Andy Griffith and Barney Fife chat with each citizen every day. Aunt Bea, Goober and the other townspeople are always willing to lend their neighbors a helping hand.

Upholding justice from the rustic, one-room jailhouse, characters of "The Andy Griffith Show" were perhaps some of America's first role models for community policing. The sleepy little town of Mayberry epitomized the essence of community policing: knowing the citizens and understanding their needs.

In stark contrast to Mayberry is a real-life town that never sleeps, Las Vegas, where community policing is not quite so easy. This racy desert oasis has more to contend with than a handful of citizens and a few small businesses. Flashy casinos and glamorous nightclubs line "the Strip," where gambling and high stakes are the first order of business for thousands of tourists.

But beyond the Strip's bright lights and neon promises is a place well over half a million people call home. And though it is no easy task, these citizens struggle to know their neighbors, and the police force tries to understand their needs.

Through the 1980s, the Las Vegas Metropolitan Police Department (Metro) considered itself an aggressive agency and was, as Undersheriff Eric Cooper stated, "a faceless entity within the community." Several Metro members described their policing philosophy as one in which police officers "kicked ass and took names." There was an "us vs. them" mentality among police officers and citizens. Today, local government, including Metro, is committed to being a significant community component that fosters a safer and healthier environment. Metro's self-image is no longer that of a schoolyard bully. Teamwork and partnership are now the watchwords that guide its decisions.

As part of that commitment, in 1989, Metro developed the line solution policing (LSP) program to address narcotics and gang activity on Las Vegas' west side. The LSP concept was a departure from traditional policing for Metro. LSP officers were charged with using innovative, proactive methods to eliminate repeat calls for service and with empowering citizens to solve problems. LSP teams were authorized to tackle problems in targeted areas by using a carefully balanced combination of enforcement and prevention approaches to crime reduction. LSP teams originally focused on identifying root social causes of crime, but they later concentrated primarily on reducing serious crime and apprehending offenders through rather traditional policing approaches.

Metro adopted the community policing philosophy after the 1992 Rodney King verdict sparked major civil unrest on Las Vegas' west side. West side residents are predominantly black, and many live in the public housing developments where the riots occurred. As Cooper stated, "We are leaning towards community policing because of the riots . . . and it is primarily for the minority community."

While definitions of community policing within Metro ranged from foot patrol programs to the coproduction of public safety with the community, almost everyone interviewed strongly believed in community policing's underlying concepts and in its potential to reduce crime-related problems in the Las Vegas metropolitan area.

However, several internal and external forces plagued Metro as it struggled to implement a community policing approach. The civil unrest, racial issues, recent population boom, election for a new sheriff, undeveloped management systems, fairly young and inexperienced personnel, citizen demands for more and different services, and struggle to blend traditional and nontraditional police services were but a few of the challenges Metro faced in implementing community policing.

THE CITY OF LAS VEGAS

Nevada's largest jurisdiction, Clark County, sprawls over 7,500 square miles and has a population of about 1.1 million. Las Vegas covers a mere 53 square miles of Clark County's desert expanse, but it is home to almost 70 percent of the county's population. The Las Vegas valley is one of the fastest-growing metropolitan areas in the United States, expanding by about 5,000 people a month. Demographically, Las Vegas is 72 percent white, 13 percent Hispanic, 11 percent black, and 4 percent American Indian and Asian.

In 1973, the Las Vegas Police Department and Clark County Sheriff's Department merged to form the Las Vegas Metropolitan Police Department. Metro provides most of the law enforcement-related sheriff functions for Clark County—but Las Vegas is the focal point for the police services Metro delivers.

Both the city of Las Vegas and Clark County finance Metro on a percentage basis determined by a formula using calls for service, population and other factors. For the most part, Metro is autonomous and establishes its own goals regarding the delivery of police services. Bill Noonan, the Las Vegas city manager, stated, "Every year, we write Metro a $43 million check, and we are not sure how the money is spent." Government leaders, including Noonan, said Metro is very cooperative in trying to solve community issues, and, according to Las Vegas Mayor Jan Laverty-Jones, "there is a tremendous amount of coordination between Metro and other city departments."

Interstate 15 winds through the middle of Las Vegas, creating a geographical boundary for Metro and dividing the city into east and west sections. However, the separation is more than geographical. The west side is a socioeconomically deprived area where citizens see themselves as isolated from the Las Vegas mainstream. According to a citywide survey Metro conducted in 1990, most Las Vegas residents felt safe within their communities, but 75 percent had changed their lifestyles due to fear of crime. While the survey indicated that most people believed Metro was doing an "excellent" or "good" job, the black community did not share those sentiments.

The relationship between west side residents and the police has worsened due to some recent events. In July 1990, Metro was criticized after three officers entered a black casino floorman's apartment and put him in a fatal headlock. In April 1992, riots sparked by the Rodney King verdict in a predominantly black west side area left relationships between blacks and the police hostile and tense. Fires, attacks on the police, sniper fire, and other offenses occurred at this time. In addition, in February 1993, two officers shot and killed a black man who threatened them with a knife.

When Metro officers were interviewed in February 1993, most felt a repeat of the 1992 rioting was inevitable. But like Los Angeles, Las Vegas was spared any riots after officers involved in the Rodney King beating were found guilty. However, the tension between the police and the minority community remained in Las Vegas, as it did in Los Angeles. Residents had observed Metro's special units performing tactical maneuvers in preparation for the "inevitable" riots. Chester Richardson, vice president of the local NAACP, said, "There's such a desperation here, wanting not just to preserve peace, but to preserve hope."

A veritable paradox existed for Metro. While the agency was trying to adopt a community policing philosophy in response to its perceived poor relationship with the minority community, it was also preparing for major civil unrest in that same community. Said Cooper, "I'm concerned that one event . . . will set back relations with the black community." Cooper also indicated that Metro officers felt stressed and fearful as a result of the mounting tension between the minority community and the police. And it was in this environment that Metro was implementing community policing.

Tourism is the lifeblood of the area's economy, as Las Vegas has 23 million visitors annually. Because tourism is the dominant industry, it is a major factor in most political decisions. This can be seen in the way the city dealt with the 1992 riots. The ordeal was termed "America's best-kept secret," according to Cooper. Had the media publicized the civil unrest, it would no doubt have had a negative impact on the tourist industry.

Policing Las Vegas had grown steadily more complex and demanding over the years leading up to the advent of LSP. Mirroring the large growth in the city's population, crime had steadily increased, with gang-related crime (narcotics trafficking and shootings) becoming the community's and the police's number one concern. Homicides, robberies, assaults, and other violent crimes had also increased substantially in the late 1980s and early 1990s.

THE LAS VEGAS METROPOLITAN POLICE DEPARTMENT

There are over 2,200 authorized positions within the Las Vegas Metropolitan Police Department, a nationally accredited agency. Approximately 1,080 are commissioned (1.67 per 1,000 population). The remaining staff consists of civilian support and detention personnel. The sheriff, administrative staff and investigation unit are located at City Hall in downtown Las Vegas. The majority of the field services division (patrol) personnel work out of four area command substations.

Sheriff John Moran had been Metro's chief executive officer since the early 1980s. Many people described Moran as the most powerful political figure in Nevada, even though he would not talk to the media and had little or no relationship with the city or county government. He epitomized and personified Metro's autonomous nature. Fiscally, he answered to no one but the voters every four years at election time. But he remained popular with his constituents and was highly respected by the vast majority of Metro personnel interviewed. According to several Metro officials, Moran had been very supportive of innovative solutions to crime problems. His term as sheriff was to expire in 1994, and he did not intend to run for a fourth term. Moran's top priorities in 1993 included

- adding 300 more police officers to Metro to properly implement community policing,

- developing a closer working relationship with the community, and

- tackling gang and illegal narcotics problems.

Metro subdivides its jurisdiction into four area commands based on workload and geographical boundaries. A captain heads each subdivision. Metro planned to reorganize its field services division so that each area command would consist of three sectors, each headed by a lieutenant. Each sector would have an LSP team, along with officers who responded to calls for service. Supplementing the beat patrol officers were several specialized units, such as the gang unit and bicycle patrol.

LINE SOLUTION POLICING

In early 1989, Metro focused on a serious problem facing the community: obvious decay and disorder in certain neighborhoods. Several apartment complexes were riddled with gang activity and gang-related crime. This placed a heavy burden on police resources, evidenced by a disparate number of service calls to these locations. Metro decided that a large influx of resources would not solve the problem, and called for an innovative approach that included citizen involvement. After coordinating with various government officials and other community leaders, Moran initiated line solution policing in July 1989.

The LSP concept was, in part, a spin-off of the tactics Metro's successful neighborhood police team used in a gang-infested public housing development. Establishing a police substation in the neighborhood had proved effective in restoring security to the fear-ridden community.

LSP teams consisted of five or six officers and one sergeant, and they were formed with existing resources at each of Metro's 1989 area commands. LSP officers were generally not responsible for radio-dispatched calls. Instead, they were expected to identify crime-related problems, develop plans to minimize or resolve the problems, and ensure that solutions were implemented.

LSP teams had programs and tactics tailored to meet each command area's unique demands. Area commanders selected LSP team members from a group of officers who had expressed a willingness to use unconventional policing methods to solve problems. Each officer attended a two-day preparatory seminar presented by Metro that emphasized problem-oriented policing (POP). Team members, working flexible hours, had the authority to identify problems and use existing resources as necessary.

In the beginning, LSP was driven by two primary objectives. First, officers were to take appropriate action to reduce non-police-related calls regarding loud parties, parking problems, speeding, and similar concerns in areas in which calls for service were atypically high. Taking "appropriate action" meant matching the resources of both government and nongovernment agencies to problems officers and citizens identified. The LSP officers' role was to accelerate responses to community problems. For example, if an area needed new lighting, LSP teams would ensure that the city installed that lighting. Metro believed that targeting high-call areas and involving citizens in the process would better prepare citizens to handle civil matters by themselves in the future. Second, officers were to assist field and investigative personnel in targeting criminals and known crime locations.

Planning for LSP continued as the program evolved from 1989 to 1993. Due to staffing shortages and service demands, LSP developed primarily into several special enforcement units concerned more with apprehending criminals than with identifying the root causes of the problems. Lt. Dennis Cobb, watch commander for the southeast area command, stated, "LSP is essentially enforcement." Several officers, including a senior patrol officer, said, "LSP has turned into a narcotics unit." A sergeant added that LSP seemed to have shifted in focus "because guys like making arrests and counting arrests."

Confusion about the exact definitions and dimensions of community policing existed at all levels of the department, but especially among patrol officers. A few department members believed the confusion was cause for concern. Cliff Davis, a black lieutenant who had been put in charge of the west Las Vegas neighborhood where the riots occurred, stated, "One of our problems is that we don't make a distinction between line solution policing, problem-oriented policing or community policing." Walt Myers, field services deputy chief, concurred. "The perception of what community policing is is our biggest concern," he said.

In 1993, community policing in Metro was still in fledgling form and, by several accounts, more talk than walk. The notion of service for citizens and more intimate organizational interaction with the community was evolving. Metro members at all levels espoused the idea that they needed to get more involved with the community. They suggested several ways to minimize the differences between the police and the community, such as assigning officers to foot patrols, having officers get out of their cars more often, and encouraging personnel to attend community meetings.

Metro did not have a set of strategies for developing and implementing community policing. Myers said, "We need to create a five-year plan . . . and we need to formalize community policing within Metro." Although Metro had a planning bureau, Myers delegated the development of the community policing implementation plan to a field services division lieutenant, giving him several weeks to complete it.

The centerpiece of Metro's plan to implement community policing in west Las Vegas was Davis. It was believed that Davis, because of the relationships he had developed with the area businesspeople and because he is black, could serve as a link between the police and the west Las Vegas residents and effectively lead the community policing initiative in that area.

VALUE-BASED MANAGEMENT

Large plaques stating Metro's fundamental values hang on every substation's walls and in strategic areas around headquarters. The impetus for the development of the values came from Cooper and Cobb, who believed the department needed several statements to reflect its core values. Before the values were developed, Metro had a short, nondescript mission statement. Cooper coordinated the work of several Metro personnel, who, in 1992, developed the department's values. Once the values were in draft form, about 30 people reviewed and refined them, putting them into final form. The purpose of the statement of values, according to Cooper, was to help the department make the "shift from a crime-fighting agency to a community service agency." It was believed that the fundamental values would become the force that directed the development of Metro's other systems. Metro's fundamental values are as follows:

> We believe the People are the source of police authority, and that our Department exists as custodian of that authority through public trust. So far as possible, we reflect community priorities while working to meet our responsibilities, and we respond to well-founded criticism with a willingness to change.

> We believe people in our community are entitled to safety and freedom from fear. We are committed to protecting them from crime, and we recognize that policing is the concern of everyone in the community, that the public and police share responsibility for protecting and improving the quality of community life.

> We believe in the dignity of all people, and recognize our responsibility to treat them with courtesy. In conflict, we must act with professional calm, common sense and sound judgment, particularly when provoked; when we must use force, it will be only that necessary to accomplish our lawful duties. We will never tolerate the abuse of police powers entrusted us by our community.

> Working to meet our responsibilities without favor or prejudice, we respect the Constitutional Rights of every person, regardless of their situation. The foundation of policing, and all American government, is the People, and we hold dear the principles embodied in the United States Constitution.

PLANNING

Crime analysis, a section within the planning bureau, worked closely with the LSP teams, but almost exclusively in tracking crime trends and identifying repeat offenders. Crime analyst Kurt Zimmer stated that each area command had one or two designated scanners, police officers assigned to be "the eyes and ears of the beat officers." According to Zimmer, the scanners were implementing POP using the SARA problem-solving model. The SARA model directs police officers to scan the environment and identify a problem, analyze the factors that contribute to the problem, respond with a targeted solution, and assess the results of the implemented solution. The scanners attended community meetings and worked with property owners and public housing development managers to deal with gangs and narcotics trafficking.

TRAINING

Lt. Jim Chaney coordinated training within Metro. At the time of the site visit, Chaney believed Metro was in the process of converting to a community policing philosophy, but he had not received direction regarding the development of a training curriculum that would support community policing.

POP was being taught as a "specialized training" course (3.5 hours long) in the basic academy; during the course, officers were introduced to the SARA model. Herman Goldstein's book, *Problem-Oriented Policing,* was required reading in the basic academy. The basic academy also provided 24.5 hours of instruction in conflict management, cultural awareness and public speaking, which, Chaney believed, supported the department's community policing initiative.

All commissioned personnel were required to receive a minimum of 24 hours of training each year. A minimum of 12 of the 24 hours had to be spent on new training. There were no required courses for personnel, with the exception of cultural awareness training. In-service training options included classes or seminars on communication skills, Spanish language skills and community-oriented policing (COP).

After the 1992 civil unrest, about 20 Metro members attended a train-the-trainer class on verbal judo, a skill Metro believed would help officers stay calm and professional under verbal assault. It was intended that those 20 would teach other Metro members what they learned in the class.

LSP training was informal. Davis, who headed the community policing effort in west Las Vegas, stated, "I started at the grass roots, reading books by Robert Trojanowicz and the IACP [International Association of Chiefs of Police] on community policing and problem-oriented policing." Davis said he had not received any formal training regarding problem-oriented or community policing from the department.

Sgt. Jeff Russo, who had been in charge of an LSP team since June 1992, said he had read the book *Beyond 911* but had not received any training in POP. Other Metro members had received some pertinent training. LSP Officer Tony Morales had received three days of community policing training from IACP. Prior to 1993, IACP had provided three days of in-service community policing training to Metro personnel who volunteered for the classes. Before 1993, few officers who were not LSP team members received any training in community policing concepts.

Lt. Terry Lesney, the Field Training and Evaluation Program (FTEP) coordinator, said, "Our department is in the learning phase of problem-oriented policing and community policing." She believed she was selected as the FTEP coordinator because she is proactive and has experience teaching POP. Myers indicated to her that he wanted to infuse POP into the FTEP.

Lesney conducted the 3.5-hour block of POP training in the basic academy, focusing on the SARA model, and she coordinated with other lieutenants who provided a four-hour block of POP training to field training officer sergeants. In 1993, a 10-hour block on POP was being put together for the entire field services division staff. Lesney had also been charged with integrating basic POP tenets into the critical tasks that new FTEP recruits needed to understand and perform. Lesney said she taught POP within a community policing philosophy framework. By that she meant that she instructed officers to form partnerships with citizens to identify and solve underlying social and crime problems.

PROMOTION AND SELECTION

Moran made it clear that the successful candidate for promotion would be knowledgeable about and supportive of line solution and community policing. *Beyond 911* was required reading for the written promotional exam; approximately two out of 100 questions covered material in the book. During the oral interview, the candidate was presented with a problem-solving scenario and was asked about his or her support and understanding of LSP. Internal affairs Sgt. Larry Espinosa said his pending promotion to lieutenant was due, in part, to his support of LSP.

The promotional process was geared toward selecting candidates who could coach and empower their subordinates, who, in turn, would then be able to direct their own activities, according to Cooper. Several department members said the key to developing a community policing ideology in their agency would be the careful selection of organizational leaders—leaders who reflected the community policing philosophy.

Metro was subject to a consent decree mandating that the department racially reflect the community it serves. Richard Myers, head of the personnel division, stated that Metro was targeting minority and female recruits and was also trying to hire officers who would be community-minded problem solvers. Myers said candidates' COP characteristics were identified through the psychological exam and oral board portion of the selection process.

LEADERSHIP

Metro managers frequently used the word "empowerment." They clearly expected independence and autonomous thinking. The area command captains had the authority to manage their areas in accordance with community needs. However, some members of the lower ranks perceived inconsistencies in how they planned and implemented LSP.

Managers were highly complimentary of the leadership philosophy Metro was promoting. Many believed they had more impact on decisions and were "freer" to be innovative in their work. The entrepreneurial spirit was also evident in the LSP officers. Morales said his sergeant was very supportive of his decisions. He felt entrusted to do what he believed was necessary in his assignment.

CALL MANAGEMENT SYSTEM

Although the call volume decreased between 1990 and 1993, with partial credit given to LSP's impact, Metro faced the same dilemma many other police departments face—finding time to adequately answer calls for service. Cobb said, "We still foster dependency in the community by use of 911." Response time was still a political issue in Las Vegas. According to administrative services Deputy Chief Richard Winget, "Metro has gotten beat up in the past regarding response time."

Metro administrators believed officers had minimal amounts of uncommitted patrol time to conduct POP activities; one deputy chief estimated that 11 percent of their time was uncommitted. Actual uncommitted patrol time seemed to vary from one area command to another. Patrol officers in the southeast area command estimated that 25 to 40 percent of their shift was uncommitted. During ride-alongs in west Las Vegas, officers indicated they would like to do more POP but did not have the time to do it effectively.

Karen Layne, the planning and research director, said Metro's last study on uncommitted patrol time was conducted in 1984. At the time of the site visit, administrators were researching strategies to prioritize calls for service and use other Metro resources for report taking. Both Myers and Winget coordinated this project and indicated Metro would implement an upgraded differential patrol response procedure sometime in 1993. They believed that if differential response were properly implemented, more Metro officers could practice LSP. As part of Metro's differential police response, Myers and Winget expected to both civilianize the report-taking process and prioritize calls. Winget indicated there were no plans to involve citizens in the development of the new differential response procedure.

MARKETING LSP AND COMMUNITY POLICING

Metro produces several informational publications for citizens and, in 1992, developed a "Tell Metro What You Think" brochure to encourage citizens to suggest improvements, compliment employees and register complaints. The brochure was available at the area commands and headquarters.

Metro conducts a six-week citizens academy seven times a year. According to Moran, the academy has been very well-received by the community. It has also been a tremendous help to the department in developing a closer relationship with citizens.

Metro did not have a comprehensive plan for marketing line solution or community policing to community members. However, according to Carri Geer, a police beat reporter for the *Las Vegas Review Journal,* Metro "is much more accessible" to the press than it has been in the past. Metro has occasionally used the media to publicize LSP accomplishments. At the time of this writing, Metro had one public information officer. Myers thought Metro should have two or three people assigned to media relations to facilitate the marketing of community policing, and he said he would recommend hiring or reassigning additional personnel to staff the public information office.

The friction between the minority community and the police department made it difficult for Metro to convince the community that the agency wanted to form partnerships with citizens to solve community problems. Geer said she had participated in ride-alongs with Metro officers to see how they carried out LSP. She wrote a series of articles in August 1992 describing her experiences. The articles outlined the progress black residents and the police had made in developing a cooperative relationship, dealing with crime and revitalizing neighborhoods in west Las Vegas. Geer said that although Moran did not talk to the press, other Metro officials, particularly Cooper and Lt. Carl Fruge, the public information officer, were very accessible.

RECOGNITION AND AWARDS

Metro has a policy that addresses department commendations and service awards, and it recognizes members for successful LSP work. Commendable actions are acknowledged in a monthly administrative notice distributed to all personnel. Metro also recognizes citizens for assisting other citizens or the police department.

CITIZEN PARTICIPATION AND POLICY DEVELOPMENT

In 1993, citizens were just beginning to participate in the development of the policies and systems that drive Metro. Although no formal mechanism existed that provided an avenue for citizens to express their opinions regarding policy development, Metro had developed several programs that involved citizens. Metro created the Use-of-Force Board, which consisted of a deputy chief, three police officers and four citizens who reviewed citizen allegations of excessive force. The Use-of-Force Board was not popular among police officers. Andy Anderson, president of the Police Protective Association, believed the board was the administration's way of appeasing the minority community.

High-ranking Metro officials serve on the Police-Community Relations Board, which meets once a month to discuss ongoing issues, particularly issues in the minority community. In 1992, the board settled on a 12-point plan to improve police-community relations that included an agreement that officers would not force suspects into a spread-eagle position.

Davis stated that either he or members of his staff meet with representatives of the west Las Vegas Housing Authority and Tenant Councils each month to discuss problems regarding abandoned cars, street cleanup, lighting, etc. Metro entered into partnership agreements with the Housing Authority and Tenant Councils that clearly defined expectations for both the police and the citizen groups. Davis made it clear that the police's "telling [citizens] what we are going to do is not going to work in my area. It is paramount the police go to the people and listen to them." However, many Metro personnel seemed reluctant to cede significant control to the community in setting departmental priorities. Said one high-ranking official, "We tend to tell the public what we think the problems are, when we should be asking the public what they want us to do."

METRO'S INTERACTION WITH OTHER AGENCIES

Several members at all levels within Metro said the level of cooperation between city and county agencies and the police department was excellent with respect to LSP efforts. Mayor Laverty-Jones and City Manager Noonan confirmed this assessment. LSP officers were encouraged through training and their supervisors to seek out help from other agencies to solve community problems.

As part of the LSP program, the southwest area command implemented a project called Community 89109. The number 89109 is the zip code of a Las Vegas district that deteriorated in the 1980s into an economically deprived, drug-infested, high-crime area.

Through Metro officers' efforts, 86 different public and private agencies participated in revitalizing the area. Community 89109 was intended to establish one or more community centers, develop a collaborative effort with public schools using the community centers, conduct positive-modeling activities for youths, and develop additional services for families, consistent with the "one-stop-shopping" concept.

This collaborative effort, considered a success by Metro members and the mayor, resulted in the procurement of two buildings in the area. One was to be the community center, and one was to house several local government service offices, such as for the police, parks and recreation, and Nevada Partners, a job training and placement service. A four-officer bike team worked the target area. Their role was to provide police services to the area, serve as a deterrent to drug sales, and frequent the Boy's Club and community center to interact with the kids as mentors. In July 1993, Community 89109 completed its first year. Further plans were being developed to coordinate activities through the University of Nevada at Las Vegas. Metro evaluated the results of Community 89109 through a series of grant-funded surveys. The survey results will provide future direction for the project.

LSP officers worked directly with the public works, fire department and city council members to resolve issues. Morales said he worked with other agencies to revitalize a neighborhood. "Public works is sandblasting the graffiti from the sidewalks and repairing broken windows, and the fire department is repainting fire hydrants," he said. Beat officers seldom interacted with other agencies in the same way the LSP officers did, however.

DEVELOPMENT NEEDS AND STRENGTHS OF LSP AND COMMUNITY POLICING

Deputy Chief Myers said departmental communication, both formal and informal, needed attention. At the time of the site visit, Myers met with the captains once a month and provided them with pertinent information. Several department members commented that communication about goals was inconsistent and fragmented. To some, LSP seemed more like a "flavor of the month club" program. A communication breakdown also existed regarding the specialization of units, according to some officers. One officer said he was not informed about special ongoing surveillances until he drove his police car into an area tactical units were observing.

RESULTS AND COMMUNITY PERCEPTIONS OF LSP AND COMMUNITY POLICING

Several successes have been documented since the adoption of LSP in 1989. Numerous neighborhoods and parks have been taken from marauding gangs and given back to citizens. Public housing developments have been purged of narcotics trafficking and gangs. Metro's efforts during the Gerson Park Project received honorable mention from *Parade Magazine*'s Exemplary Law Enforcement Program, which identifies initiatives that provide outstanding service to the community. Several businesses, including bars and motels that were generating up to 100 calls a month, have been closed or are working with Metro to reduce crime-related problems. The Community Accident Reduction Effort (CARE) has reduced the number of accidents at major intersections.

Metro has one of the premier bicycle units in the United States. It is primarily responsible for patrolling the Strip and the downtown casino area. Traffic is near gridlock at these locations, and bicycle unit officers are much quicker to respond to citizens in need, having easier access to the trouble spots. As a result of Metro's additions to the bicycle patrol, reported crime has decreased in these areas.

From 1989 to April 1992, the relationship between the police and the minority community improved, as citizens realized they would directly benefit from the LSP program. Unfortunately, since the 1992 civil unrest, tension had mounted once again. As mentioned earlier, the 1993 shooting of a black man by two white officers had worsened relations. Unknown snipers had recently fired at Metro's southeast area command substation.

Noonan believed police-community relations were on the upswing, based on the fact that he was not getting as many letters from citizens about the department as he previously had. But Laverty-Jones believed the minority community "has a real suspicion of the police," even though Metro has done some innovative things in predominantly black neighborhoods. Chester Richardson, vice president of the local NAACP, did not believe community policing was being implemented in west Las Vegas' economically deprived sections. He felt that "Lt. Davis isn't the [sole] answer" to implementing community policing in the area. Richardson believed community policing involves developing partnerships with the community and the media, and he indicated that such partnerships had not been formed in west Las Vegas.

Several Metro members believed the black leaders who represented west Las Vegas residents had their own agendas and were aggravating an already bad situation. Noonan thought that the city's black leaders were not as hostile as they had once been and that, by 1993, minority representatives were working cooperatively with the city government and Metro.

THE FUTURE

Many unanswered questions remained regarding the direction Metro would take in the future. No one person or group believed they could accurately forecast what would happen to the agency. Moran did not plan to run for another term in office. The undersheriff and two assistant sheriffs planned to retire when Moran left office, creating vacancies in the top four Metro positions.

In 1993, Metro promoted the Neighborhood-Oriented Police Protection and Enforcement (NOPPE) referendum to add 300 more police officers, increase the number of neighborhood substations and expand the jail. Metro billed NOPPE as a program to develop a partnership between neighborhood citizens and the police officers assigned to those neighborhoods. Metro asked for citizen support for the referendum to "identify the criminals, catch the criminals and get the criminals off your neighborhood streets."

Laverty-Jones said she believed 7,000 to 8,000 entry-level jobs would open up once three large motels were built on the Strip in 1994. She and other government officials hammered out an agreement with the motel owners to earmark those jobs exclusively for west Las Vegas' unemployed residents. While details had not been developed, it was believed that providing so many jobs to people in economically deprived sections of Las Vegas would help to revitalize those areas.

There were several Metro members who could be characterized as load-pulling spirits—leaders of the transition who would help move Metro from primarily practicing traditional policing to primarily practicing nontraditional community policing. There were also many department members who might not play a leadership role in the transition, but who cared, were energetic and had the skills and abilities to lessen the differences between Metro and the citizens it serves. But most of all, they believed they could make a difference.

Las Vegas is no Mayberry. Television made policing look easy, but what about reality? It is difficult, as Metro realized, to get back to the basics when dealing with a thriving, complex metropolis as opposed to a fictitious small town. Despite the complexities of modern-day life, Metro members were trying to get in touch with their community by getting to know their neighbors and understanding their needs.

POSTSCRIPT

In the summer of 1993, the department abandoned its LSP program. The agency's leadership decided the special-unit approach to community policing would never enable the department to fundamentally change the way it did business. At the time LSP was discontinued, department spokespeople indicated that the agency's ultimate goal was for all patrol officers to practice POP.

The Evolution of Community Policing in Newport News, Va.

by Lynn Babcock

INTRODUCTION

Lt. Mo Mowry, a 26-year veteran of the Newport News, Va., Police Department and the head of the property crimes unit, recently decided to take a different approach to addressing daytime residential burglaries in the city. From past experience, Mowry knew that most of these burglaries occurred during the school year, and he believed juveniles were responsible. To be certain, he carefully analyzed departmental data and determined that there was a correlation between juveniles who were not in school and a series of daytime break-ins in residential neighborhoods. He then identified juveniles who had skipped school during the first month after summer vacation, checked their criminal histories and began methodically creating a database on these individuals. The database included information on their schools, grade levels and residences.

Now, whenever a daytime residential burglary is reported to the department, Mowry checks his database for information on previously truant juveniles who live in that neighborhood. A department detective then checks with school officials to determine whether any of the potential suspects did not attend all of their classes on the day of the burglary. (From earlier research, Mowry had learned that truant juveniles often attend their first class so they will be recorded in attendance for the entire day.)

Using a problem-solving model, Mowry thoroughly analyzed the problem and tailored a response based on his analysis. Although he did not formally assess the response's impact on the burglary problem, it appeared that clearance rates for the burglaries increased. Mowry was also convinced that his database would be a deterrent to future burglaries, as the truant juveniles knew he had cataloged their names, addresses and histories.

It was no surprise to the Newport News Police Department that a detective would develop an innovative response to an ongoing crime problem. The department pioneered the development of a problem-solving model for police in 1984. Since then, the department has established a number of mechanisms for its departmentwide problem-oriented policing (POP) initiative. These support mechanisms include the formation of the Problem Analysis Advisory Committee (PAAC) to assist officers with POP projects; the addition of a problem-solving component to field training, as well as annual qualifying and promotional exams that test officers' knowledge of and experience with POP; and the establishment of a specialty pay grade for those with excellent problem-solving skills.

Over the years, and as the department's leadership has changed, both the concept and the practice of POP have evolved in Newport News. By 1993, the POP process had become an informal practice for many officers. For example, an officer who noticed that police were often called to a loud nightclub might work with Alcoholic Beverage Control officials to tighten enforcement there. In doing so, the officer might not use every step of a formal problem-solving model to analyze and address the problem; the officer might use the model to think through the problem and develop a response. It is likely that the officer would not formally document such a process. Various police department personnel estimated that 60 to 70 percent of the agency's officers now take this informal approach to problem solving, bypassing PAAC and other means of formal analysis and documentation.

This approach to policing reflects the views of the agency's leadership. Jay Carey, the Newport News police chief from 1986 to 1994, believed the police have to go beyond just solving problems and actually formalize community-police interaction. Under Carey's vision of policing, known as "neighborhood policing," 24-hour responsibility for patrol areas was transferred from captains to lieutenants, and officers were assigned to smaller fixed geographical beats so they could get to know citizens and neighborhood problems better. In his view, implementing neighborhood policing was the next logical step for policing in Newport News.

THE CITY OF NEWPORT NEWS

Newport News, a city of 175,000, is located in what is referred to as Virginia's Hampton Roads region. Situated to the south and east of Richmond, the state capital, Newport News is clustered among a group of medium-sized cities that make up a metropolitan area of about 2 million people. Located on a peninsula, the city is 22 miles long and 4 miles wide. Newport News' downtown area is divided by a railroad and an interstate highway system, isolating the mostly African-American residents of the southeast community from the businesses and government agencies on the other side.

Newport News has been one of the nation's shipbuilding centers for many years. At one time, various shipbuilding companies employed over 30,000 people in Newport News. Between 1989 and 1993, however, the shipyard laid off 6,000 workers, and the local unemployment rate rose from 4 to 7 percent. In an effort to be less dependent on the shipbuilding industry, the city has been working to attract several more large companies. While the largest industry in Newport News is blue-collar, the majority of the residents (66%) hold white-collar jobs. Blue-collar workers make up the remaining 34 percent. Per capita income is $16,000, and the median household income is $37,535.[1]

Like many communities nationwide, Newport News was adversely impacted by the national recession that took place in the early 1990s. In 1991, the city implemented an austerity program to minimize discretionary expenditures and significantly reduce capital expenditures. Despite the need for the austerity program, the city's overall economic condition remained sound; Newport News consistently maintained Aa- and AA-bond ratings from Moody's Investor Services and Standard & Poor's during the late 1980s and early 1990s. During the same period, the city experienced slow economic growth that paralleled its slow but steady population growth.

Newport News is demographically diverse. Sixty-two percent of residents are white, 33 percent are African American, 3 percent are Hispanic, and 2 percent are Asian. Police department personnel are somewhat less diverse: 80 percent of the agency's sworn employees are white, 17 percent are African American, 2 percent are Hispanic, and 1 percent are Asian. The department has two distinct patrol divisions: north and south. Seventy-three percent of the citizens in north patrol are white, and a majority of the citizens in south patrol are black.

The Newport News city government fared well in a 1989 survey of city residents. Residents were generally content with the services various city departments provided. Garbage collection ranked the highest of city services. The police department also received positive ratings in the survey.

The police department has the same concerns and headaches that most large police departments do. Assistant Chief Joe Gaskins attributes some of the increases in the city's crime, particularly violent crimes, to the migration of drug dealers and gang members to Newport News from cities to the north.

The department has a uniformed strength of almost 300, which equates to an estimated 1.7 officers per 1,000 population, but agency personnel acknowledge staff limitations in handling calls for service. The department's call load rose significantly in the late 1980s and early 1990s. In 1988, the department received just under 260,000 calls for service; by 1993, it received over 325,000—an increase of 25 percent. Department officials attributed the increase to

---

1. Office of Public Information and Community Relations, *City of Newport News Performance Report*, 1991, p. 14.

greater vigilance by Crimewatch, a community crime prevention organization, increased citizen fear levels and steady population growth.

PROBLEM-SOLVING SUPPORT STRUCTURE

In March 1983, Darrel Stephens became the first Newport News police chief to be appointed from outside the department. Stephens' appointment followed a study by an outside consultant that recommended a laundry list of changes to strengthen the department's administration. The study was commissioned by the city manager, who was concerned about reports of officers' using excessive force and inappropriately using firearms.

Soon after Stephens took the helm, the department began developing a new set of policies and procedures. While the main goal was to update operating procedures that were over a decade old and often in conflict with the general orders manual, the department was also preparing for accreditation, which it received in March 1986.[2]

Many operational changes occurred in the agency during Stephens' tenure. During 1983 and 1984, the department eliminated weekly rotating shifts in favor of fixed, 12-month shifts; doubled the amount of in-service training from 40 hours every other year to 40 hours each year; implemented a new performance evaluation system that included an annual qualifying exam; and adopted a college requirement for promotion to supervisory and management positions. All of these changes were implemented with the goal of professionalizing the department.

These changes were accomplished with a dramatic change in the department's management style. Stephens established committees that allowed greater input into decision-making and encouraged thinking that was "outside of the lines." During this period, the department also participated in a policing experiment funded by the National Institute of Justice and carried out with assistance from the Police Executive Research Forum (PERF). Initially framed as a crime analysis experiment, the project was intended to improve patrol officers' effectiveness by helping them focus on developing solutions to recurrent problems manifested as repeat calls for service.

Under the problem-oriented policing project, an 11-member task force comprising sworn and civilian employees at all ranks developed and implemented a problem-solving model for the department. The task force began a variety of initiatives that provided structural support to problem solving in Newport News. In brief, these initiatives included the following:

Development of a Problem-Solving Model

With assistance from experts such as Herman Goldstein, a University of Wisconsin law professor, and Barry Poyner, a British crime prevention expert, the task force developed a four-step problem-solving model and an extensive guide to help officers analyze problems. The guide helped officers to systematically apply the model to crime and community problems, through the use of a checklist and a formula for action.

Provision of Training

All supervisors above the rank of sergeant received 32 hours of training in problem solving and related issues. Nineteen patrol officers and detectives also received training.

---

2. John E. Eck and William Spelman, *Problem Solving: Problem-Oriented Policing in Newport News*, Police Executive Research Forum (PERF): 1987, p. 35.

Establishment of the Problem Analysis Advisory Committee

The Problem Analysis Advisory Committee (PAAC), which ultimately replaced the task force, was established to help officers and other employees evaluate and respond to problems. The committee, which has a rotating captain as its chair, meets once a month to review problems department employees are addressing. Projects are reviewed most frequently during the initial problem-solving steps. The committee tracks POP projects to avoid duplication of efforts and allow for assessments of results. Committee members come from all ranks in the department, and they serve for one year. PAAC meetings are open and serve as a mechanism for spreading information about problem solving throughout the department.

Revision of Personnel Evaluations and Promotional Exams

Questions to assess an employee's knowledge and practice of problem solving were added to promotional exams and performance appraisals. Among qualified candidates vying for promotion, those who supported and practiced POP principles got promoted.

Designation of a POP Coordinator

The department designated one person to track problem-solving efforts, provide administrative support to the PAAC chair and maintain POP project files. Before becoming chief in 1986, Carey served as the POP coordinator. Later, POP coordinator Linda Swope, a lieutenant, spent 15 to 20 percent of her time on POP-related work, also serving as the department's accreditation manager.

Before the task force was established, the department had begun assessing whether all calls for service required a police response, and prioritizing those that did. Community service officers handled calls that did not require an officer, such as those regarding larcenies and cold burglaries, over the telephone. The department ultimately increased the number of calls handled over the telephone from 10 to 35 percent.

Many of these structural support mechanisms are still in place almost 10 years after they were implemented. Several others have been added over the last decade. Officers and supervisors must now demonstrate knowledge of problem solving to pass the annual qualifying exam, a test on which they must demonstrate their knowledge of policies and procedures. Between 25 and 40 questions on the 100- to 150-question tests concern POP. Field training officers must also have knowledge of POP and participate in POP activities to be selected to train. Master police officer (MPO), a specialty position with a rank between officer and sergeant, was created in 1986 to recognize officers who had POP skills and practiced problem solving, or who had expertise in other areas, such as field training. MPOs receive additional pay. The department also stopped requiring officers to fill out monthly activity reports that documented such traditional measures of policing as summonses issued, arrests made and accidents investigated. The monthly reports now cover progress on POP projects, enumerate neighborhood concerns and describe contacts between police, citizens and crime prevention organizations. There is no standardized format for writing the reports.

TREND TOWARD INFORMAL PROBLEM SOLVING

Although a number of structural support mechanisms for formal problem-solving efforts are in place in the agency, many department employees do not routinely practice and document formal problem solving as it was developed in the 1980s. Both those employees who have practiced POP since 1984 and officers who have joined the department since the inception of problem solving indicated that the process has become much more "informal" over the last decade.

Carey agreed that department personnel do not regularly use the formal POP model. Carey believed the problem-solving principles had become second nature to Newport News police employees. Although most officers do not document problem-solving activities, they routinely take an analytical approach to crime problems because problem solving has become ingrained in the way the department does business.

In contrast, one sergeant said most problem solving was being done by the same people who were working on problems when the study began in 1984. Capt. Janice Thurman, an original member of the task force put together by then-Chief Stephens, said, "There is a core group of people who know what problem solving means and use it." She added that those who are not in the core—about 12 people, she estimates—"pay lip service to it."

"All of the good POP projects have been done," said one patrol sergeant, explaining why few officers have undertaken full-blown POP projects in recent years. (Fifteen active POP projects were on file at the time of the site visit.) Downtown prostitution and other major crime and disorder problems had been addressed since 1984, leaving officers with smaller, less publicized problems to handle, the sergeant indicated.

Some officers seemed to formally document problem solving primarily to meet the requirements for promotion or transfer. One officer who had been with the department for over three years began documenting his problem-solving efforts via the PAAC so he would be eligible for the MPO rank. MPO candidates must have participated in a POP project within the previous three years to be promoted to that rank.

Others in the department said most police officers dislike the paperwork required to document the formal POP process. Lt. Mowry, although a strong proponent of the formal POP process, said, "The police officer's nightmare is paperwork." Assistant Chief Gaskins argued that "using POP has to be a natural process. If it's not natural, it bogs people down." Administrative personnel frequently review the problem-solving structure to determine how to make the process easier.

POP coordinator Swope worries, however, about the consequences of informal POP practices. She says those who undertake problem solving without participating in the PAAC process do not get the benefit of feedback on their efforts and interaction with command personnel. She is also troubled by the prospect that informal problem solvers tackling complex problems may shorten or skip steps in the problem-solving model if they do not think through and document actions taken during each step. In addition, Stephens said the informal approach often leads officers to apply previously used solutions to current problems, which can result in ineffective responses.

NEIGHBORHOOD POLICING

Carey was the primary impetus for the department's adoption of neighborhood policing, according to command staff, city government officials and media personnel. Carey, along with Gaskins, believed that Newport News citizens wanted more involvement with city government and the police department. Citizen activist Katherine Grayson agreed: "The community is starving for interaction." However, Gaskins also believed that many citizens were not comfortable speaking with the police officers they met on the street. No particular incidents precipitated the department's adoption of neighborhood policing. No racial, police misconduct or unnecessary-use-of-force incidents appear to have led the community to request more input in police department operations.

Carey felt that two early retirement programs and a forced reduction in management-level positions—the ranks of major and deputy chief were eliminated—also prompted the shift to neighborhood policing. Changing crime conditions in the city may also have set the stage for neighborhood policing. Crime analyst Lynn Flint indicated that crime was no longer concentrated in pockets of the city, which made it less effective for police to target just a few areas. However, one department manager believed the implementation of neighborhood policing reflected Carey's attempt to "put his name on something."

In 1989, Carey formed a study group of police employees from all ranks and sections of the department to determine the requirements for implementing neighborhood policing. Carey convened the group because the department had previously succeeded in using committees to make operational changes. This committee and several other internal entities evaluated the need for goals, ministation sites and new policies and procedures for neighborhood policing.

Carey also contracted with Robert Wasserman, a consultant, to develop a model department personnel could use to determine how much uncommitted time patrol officers had each day. Carey believed that for officers to have time to work with the community to solve problems, at least 50 percent of their shift would need to be uncommitted. The study revealed that, depending on the shift and time of day, officers spent 60 to 70 percent of their time on calls for service, directed patrol or other assigned duties. Based on the uncommitted-time study and the committee's work, the department submitted a three-year budget request for approximately $1 million to the city council in 1990. Department officials indicated that the money would provide the agency with the personnel, equipment and substations needed to implement neighborhood policing in the north patrol area. The budget plan proposed giving more responsibility to captains, lieutenants, sergeants, and officers by holding them accountable for citizen satisfaction with police services in the north patrol area. The package did not receive funding that year, despite the department's efforts to educate city officials about the benefits of neighborhood policing. According to Assistant City Manager Bill Mitchell, the proposal was not funded because of the city's poor financial condition at the time. The city council also rejected the budget package the following year, citing the same reason.

While Carey had little luck getting the neighborhood policing budget package past the city council in 1990 or 1991, public pressure following a series of sexual assaults in the predominantly African-American southeast community may have prompted the city council to approve the hiring of additional police officers. In this instance, the police department did not report seven related incidents of molestation of young girls to Crimewatch, and they were publicly criticized for not alerting the community. At around the same time, the city council approved the hiring of more than 40 officers over a two-year budget period. The first new officers began working in the summer of 1992.

Although the department did not receive the full amount of funding Carey felt was necessary to move ahead with neighborhood policing, it began to gear up for the change anyway, starting in the north patrol area. (The north patrol area, which encompasses roughly the northern two-thirds of the city, was selected as the pilot implementation area because it generated fewer calls for service than south patrol and was less densely populated. The command staff believed it would be easier to work out any bugs in the implementation of neighborhood policing in north patrol before implementing it in south patrol.)

In the summer of 1991, following the rejection of the 1992 budget proposal, Carey transferred several lieutenants to north patrol. Along with the captain of north patrol, these lieutenants were assigned to implement neighborhood policing in that area. Lacking additional funds for any changes, Carey simply told his staff to "be creative" and to aim for implementing neighborhood policing in north patrol some six months later.

The lieutenants gave much of the responsibility for planning for neighborhood policing to committees of sergeants, MPOs and patrol officers working in the patrol area. Each committee evaluated and suggested changes in the beat boundaries, the job descriptions, the bid shift system, and other pertinent areas that would be affected by the shift to neighborhood policing.

To determine new boundary lines for beats, the crime analysis unit began evaluating data the committee gathered on neighborhood boundaries, as well as computer-aided dispatch data. The new boundaries were intended to keep "neighborhoods" intact. Once the crime analysis unit analyzed all the data, boundaries were drawn and a new officer call number system was instituted to designate each employee's shift, beat location and patrol area.

A new bidding process for shifts was also implemented. Previously, officers had bid for shifts every year; under the new system, officers bid for shifts only once every three years. This change was intended to keep officers in specific areas for longer periods of time, allowing them to get to know citizens and problems on their beats. Various committee members also began attending roll-call briefings and working group meetings to bring other employees up to date on implementation activities.

The community involvement committee was one of several committees organized for the first stage of implementation. Made up of officers and supervisors from the north patrol area, this committee was charged with exploring ways community members could contribute to problem solving under neighborhood policing. The committee suggested establishing community involvement teams (CITs), advisory boards of community leaders who would help the department set priorities for police services in north patrol. As originally conceived, there would be six CITs—one for each of the new patrol areas. CIT meetings would provide an opportunity for lieutenants and officers to hear citizens' concerns firsthand. In the past, citizens had frequently voiced their concerns to city council members, by-passing police department personnel. A list of recommended community leaders for the CITs was forwarded to Carey, who later invited them to join the effort. The north patrol area commander followed up with the new participants, stressing the department's interest in their joining the CITs.

However, several department members felt that citizens had little real involvement in planning the move to neighborhood policing. The chief told these officials that he did not think it was appropriate for the community to play a significant role in the internal planning process.

Neighborhood policing officially began in north patrol on April 1, 1992. On this date, north patrol lieutenants became responsible for one of three geographical patrol areas. Before April 1, north patrol had been divided into seven patrol areas or districts based on workload indicators. Each patrol area had three watches, each managed by a lieutenant with assistance from two or three sergeants. Captains had previously been in charge of the north and south patrol areas.

Lieutenants enthusiastically greeted the change. Said one, "It's like running your own little police department." They became more active in community meetings, handling complaints and concerns that would have normally gone directly to the chief. They also became more accessible to the public, making the community contacts that captains or the chief had made in the past.

Lieutenants reported that officers took on more responsibility and acquired a new sense of beat ownership as a result of neighborhood policing. "The officers will try to get a problem in their beat corrected before their sergeant finds out about it," said one lieutenant. Yet with respect to their day-to-day responsibilities, many patrol officers and sergeants felt little had changed with the implementation of neighborhood policing. For example, one officer said the main difference he noticed was that some of his call numbers were changed to letters.

To help ensure a smooth transition in implementing neighborhood policing in south patrol, which was scheduled for Oct. 1, 1992, north and south patrol lieutenants met regularly during the planning and implementation phases of the shift to neighborhood policing in north patrol. Thus, south patrol personnel were kept updated on the progress in north patrol, while north patrol personnel benefited from south patrol personnel's input.

A memorandum was sent to patrol officers delineating the new beat boundaries and announcing the implementation of neighborhood policing in north patrol. Other than this directive, personnel received little information about the change. Said one mid-level manager, "I don't think anybody's ever come out and said what we expect to gain [from neighborhood policing]."

Most department employees were aware of the shift to neighborhood policing, but they were confused about how it related to the department's problem-oriented approach to policing. Employee definitions of neighborhood policing included the following:

- "asking people to help identify problems"

- "a spin-off of POP"

- "going to community meetings, getting out of the patrol car"

- "smaller precincts throughout the community"

- "breaking down the 'us vs. them' mentality"

- "pushing the responsibility and accountability for the delivery of police services to the lieutenant level"

Some command staff were also unclear as to the specific direction Carey had in mind for neighborhood policing, and they informed him of their concerns. Carey indicated that he planned to clarify the goals and direction for the effort. With respect to explaining his view to command staff, Carey said the implementation of neighborhood policing was a standing item on the weekly management committee meeting agenda.

Patrol officers were not trained in neighborhood policing until April 1993, which may have contributed to some of the confusion regarding the goals for the effort. The training, which lasted eight hours, covered the general rationale for neighborhood policing: namely, that it would enable police personnel to get to know community members better, develop a better understanding of community problems, and acquire a sense of ownership of geographical areas. The training also covered problem-solving techniques, the relationship of crime analysis to neighborhood policing and community engagement skills. Finally, the training addressed what the community could expect from the police, and vice versa, as a result of the change. Additional future training blocks were to cover cultural issues as they related to neighborhood policing.

THE COMMUNITY'S ROLE

Community leader Katherine Grayson, who became involved in public safety issues after forming a grassroots community crime watch, first heard about neighborhood policing during a police-community meeting at which police told citizens that the department would be moving in that direction. To obtain more information about neighborhood policing and other police department initiatives, she made appointments with several high-ranking department officials. At these meetings, she was told of the city's "Framework for the Future," a master plan for Newport News. The plan had been created from concept papers that staff in each city agency developed and citizens later reviewed. Delineated in the master plan were such police department goals as improving citizen cooperation, communication and involvement with the police; increasing police visibility and familiarity in the neighborhoods they patrol; and increasing police staffing.

Grayson approved of the joint police-community responsibilities outlined in the plan, but she felt that the police were merely presenting their viewpoints at community meetings, rather than "probing the community" for ideas and concerns. She felt that the police were also missing opportunities to educate the community about the advantages of neighborhood policing. She believed the department should market its programs through the electronic media and encourage officers to become more involved in positive, high-profile activities, such as a dinner for the homeless that several department members had attended.

Other citizens echoed Grayson's perceptions of limited police involvement in the community. Annie Mae Williams, chairperson of one of the neighborhood crime watches, knew two of the officers who patrolled her neighborhood by name, but she said most people in her area were afraid of the police and, as a result, did not have a lot of contact with them. She realized the department could not maintain a constant presence in her neighborhood, but she wished there were more police-community interaction. She was hopeful that, in 1993, "the police department and neighborhood could really get together and just sit down and talk." Williams praised the department for participating in a recent neighborhood cleanup. During that initiative, the police chief and other city officials helped local residents pick up debris.

Williams, who was 64 and had a full-time job at the time of this writing, became a crime watch chairperson in the mid-1980s. There was a hole in her kitchen wall from a bullet that passed through her front door. She believed that someone may have fired at her house because of her activism with respect to drug dealers and crack houses. She had been working with out-of-state landlords to destroy abandoned houses used to sell drugs. She said city personnel quickly took action when neighbors notified them of problem locations. She also said drug dealers seemed to stay one step ahead of the city, moving from one run-down house to another.

ANTICRIME PARTNERSHIP PROGRAM

In late 1992, Newport News was awarded an Anticrime Partnership Program grant through the Virginia Governor's Office. While not specifically a part of the shift to neighborhood policing, the grant provided the department with additional community-oriented resources. Specifically, the grant funds were to be used to help unite police and city services, schools, utilities, and the housing authority to improve the quality of life in the southeast community, as well as decrease the fear of crime in southeast neighborhoods. The grant provided funds for hiring officers to address problems in the target areas. It also provided resources to combat problems related to parks and recreation, community services and libraries.

BARRIERS TO NEIGHBORHOOD POLICING

Several internal and external barriers seemed to inhibit progress in implementing neighborhood policing in Newport News. In addition to the training and communication concerns mentioned earlier, the department struggled with other issues.

Some of Carey's top managers were still loyal to past approaches to policing. For example, one manager said, "If POP is done right, you don't need neighborhood policing." However, while some managers might have resisted the change, they did not actively block the implementation of neighborhood policing.

Another barrier to neighborhood policing was supervisors' failure to encourage officers to engage in problem solving. Line officers throughout the department believed supervisors' level of interest in and support of POP greatly determined how much problem solving officers did. If the sergeant or lieutenant supported the problem-solving process and mentored the patrol officers, officers would identify and work on problems. However, if such support was not forthcoming, officers would do little in this regard. It was thought that few supervisors strongly supported problem-solving efforts. "There aren't that many sergeants who understand POP and give a damn about it," lamented one first-line supervisor. Sergeants had also seen few changes resulting from the implementation of neighborhood policing. Because their understanding of the new approach was limited, their ability to communicate expectations concerning the change was impeded.

An additional factor that inhibited neighborhood policing was the frequency of "cross dispatching." Sergeants mentioned that a shortage of patrol officers resulted in the dispatching of calls from one section of north patrol to officers in a different section of north patrol. Many sergeants and patrol officers felt the frequent cross dispatching made it difficult, if not impossible, for officers to get to know the people on their beat and concentrate on their concerns.

Although officers were assigned to a geographical area under neighborhood policing, detectives were not, and several department employees considered this a drawback. One captain indicated that this lack of integration had also been a concern when the department implemented POP. Cooperation between investigators and patrol officers was one of the official 1993 goals for the department.

The level of trust between citizens and the police department was not high, which may have also inhibited the implementation of neighborhood policing. Some officers believed that many in the community were too fearful of retribution from criminals to become involved in neighborhood policing efforts. In addition, the relationship between the department and the *Daily Press,* a newspaper that covers the metropolitan Newport News area, was somewhat antagonistic. It seemed that the newspaper did little to promote the department's neighborhood policing efforts.

The reporter and editor who covered the police beat were alternately bored with or suspicious of the department's problem-oriented and neighborhood policing efforts. The editor admitted that the newspaper had not reported the shift to neighborhood policing because the topic was "bland" and lacked appeal. The reporter believed problem solving was a reactionary, and ultimately temporary, police response to crime. For the first six months after she was hired in July 1992, the department's public information officer concentrated her efforts on improving police-press relations in general, rather than on marketing neighborhood policing to the media and the community. Ironically, the department seemed to be better known nationally for its innovative work on POP than it was in the city itself.

Even though Newport News had been practicing POP for 10 years, many of the nontraditional approaches that accompanied the philosophy, such as a delayed response in nonemergency cases, were still not fully supported by the public and, consequently, by elected officials. Many city officials and citizens continued to judge the department on such criteria as crime and clearance rates, rather than on the police's effectiveness in resolving crime and disorder problems—even those that were chronic and troublesome to residents. In a recent survey, citizens ranked crime the number one problem in the city, followed by education and transportation concerns.

THE FUTURE OF NEIGHBORHOOD POLICING

The Newport News Police Department has significantly improved its image with the community over the past 10 years. Before POP was first implemented, the department had a reputation for brutality. By 1988, outsiders saw the agency as a professional and progressive entity, although some still considered it to have an authoritarian streak. From 1988 to 1993, the department's reputation continued to improve, although officers were still seen as unapproachable at times.

Many believed the success of neighborhood policing rested on the hiring of additional officers. Others believed Carey needed to communicate his vision and expectations regarding neighborhood policing at every possible forum, if the approach was to be understood, adopted and practiced by most police personnel. Still others felt he should have reiterated his commitment to problem solving, lest neighborhood policing become more of a public relations effort to develop kinship with citizens than an approach to policing that would reduce crime and disorder problems. Regardless of the direction Carey or subsequent chiefs lead the department in coming years, one thing is clear: modern community policing is a dynamic operational practice that evolves over time to reflect changing community, organizational and political needs.

Community Policing in Philadelphia

by Ondra Berry

INTRODUCTION

On the evening of Feb. 9, 1993, the captain of Philadelphia's 6th Police District, John Collins, along with five uniformed officers, met with a neighborhood association in a gay and lesbian nightclub. The nightclub, just off an alley in downtown Philadelphia, was not open for entertainment but was, instead, hosting this town watch meeting to recruit local residents, many of whom were gay or lesbian, for citizen patrols. A year earlier, in response to several beatings of local residents by bar patrons, the police district had helped this citizens group organize patrols. Collins claimed these patrols had reduced crime by over 50 percent in the area, despite cutbacks in police staffing. But now that the novelty and excitement had worn off, fewer residents were conducting patrols.

On the dance floor, facing a group of about 20 residents standing around a bar counter, Collins made his pitch: "I took an officer out [of patrol], and people took back the streets and crime dropped in half. You can have more effect than the police can, and it's been proven." Behind Collins, standing around a second bar counter, were the uniformed officers, watching with their arms folded across their chests. He went on: "With town watch waning, crime is going up. More than half the crime doesn't get reported to me." Following his plea for more participation, Collins engaged the group in a discussion of the difficulties gays and lesbians face when reporting street assaults and of the need to recruit more residents to patrol the neighborhood. The meeting ended with a march through the dark neighborhood, to which Collins assigned two patrol officers.

This is a single example of how the Philadelphia Police Department was implementing community policing in 1993. Throughout the city, captains met regularly with their diverse communities—Russian Jewish immigrants, African Americans, merchants, young professionals, and others. Community policing in Philadelphia also involved the establishment of a network of storefront stations. It entailed the decentralization of many headquarters units to area and district commands. And it involved the assignment of several specialist officers, the "five squad," to districts to assist captains in preventing crime, aiding victims, cleaning up trash, removing abandoned cars, and dealing with community relations.

Community policing has changed the Philadelphia Police Department, an agency with a long history of conflict with many of its communities. This case study outlines those changes. It is based on several interviews with community members who regularly deal with the police, as well as observations of community meetings and other interactions between the police and residents. It is also based on interviews with patrol officers, district captains and senior executives. In addition, it incorporates the findings from a survey of officers the Police Executive Research Forum (PERF) conducted.

THE CITY OF PHILADELPHIA

Philadelphia is a 129-square-mile urban area with approximately 1.6 million residents. The city is about evenly split between residents of white European descent and those of other racial and cultural backgrounds. African Americans are the largest minority group, making up 40 percent of the population.

The city has a mayor-council form of government, which administered a budget of $336 million in 1993. According to 1992 figures, the police department had 6,523 sworn officers, providing a ratio of 4.1 officers per 1,000 residents. The Philadelphia Police Department is headed by a commissioner who is appointed by the mayor and who has traditionally risen from within the ranks. The rank structure, in descending order, is commissioner, deputy commissioner, chief inspector, inspector, captain, lieutenant, sergeant, corporal/detective, and officer. The police commissioner serves at the pleasure of the mayor, and the mayor, having run on a community policing platform, supports this approach.

The Philadelphia Police Department has had a troubled past. In the early years of this century, the department was ridiculed for incompetence, serving as the model for the "Keystone Cops." In later years, there were allegations of police brutality and corruption within the department. While many U.S. police agencies began to institute changes in response to the civil disturbances of the late 1960s, the Philadelphia Police Department successfully resisted doing so. During the same time, the department was rocked by a series of scandals. In 1983, a federal gambling investigation into police corruption was initiated in Philadelphia. Over 100 police officers were eventually indicted, including a deputy commissioner.

In 1985 and 1986, investigations into police attacks against handcuffed prisoners led to other indictments for narcotics-related police corruption. In May 1985, a police confrontation with an African-American religious cult (MOVE) resulted in the destruction of two city blocks by fire and the death of 11 MOVE members. The commission appointed to study the incident found that the department inappropriately handled the incident and the events leading up to it.

However, in 1986, Philadelphia was on the cusp of change. Wilson Goode, the first elected African-American mayor, was disturbed by the MOVE incident and acted to change the public perception of the police force as insensitive and intransigent. Goode appointed Kevin Tucker, the former head of the local Secret Service office, as police commissioner. Tucker was the first commissioner in the department's history who had not risen through the ranks.

Tucker created the Police Study Task Force, a blue-ribbon committee of business, civic, academic, and police leaders, to examine the police department. According to the Police Study Task Force report, the police department continued to have a negative reputation with the public. The report indicated that the department had withheld from the community information about improper police conduct, bribery, corruption, or dishonesty. This lack of information allowed citizens to develop a negative perception of the agency that was bounded by only their imaginations.

The report revealed a host of organizational deficiencies. The department was highly centralized and partitioned into many special units, most operating out of headquarters. Patrol operations were divided between the north and south patrol bureaus, headed by chief inspectors. The bureaus were divided into nine divisions, headed by inspectors. Each division was made up of two to four districts (a total of 23); districts were headed by captains. Officers were deployed on a six-days-on-duty, two-days-off-duty rotating shift schedule that ensured equal staffing 24 hours a day, seven days a week. Of police officers in the 10 largest U.S. cities, Philadelphia's were the lowest paid.

Twelve ranks separated patrol officers from the police commissioner. Promotion to any rank other than the first deputy commissioner position was controlled through the civil service process the city's personnel department administered. Because the department discriminated in hiring and promotions, several employees filed lawsuits, which resulted in a series of court decisions that mandated the use of quota systems in hiring and promoting African Americans, Hispanics and women. Promotions depended solely on seniority and test scores, and little attention had been paid to career development and in-service training.

Most managers and executives had had little exposure to the reforms other police agencies had undertaken in the previous decades. Concern over corruption had bolstered the top-down command hierarchy and stifled innovation at the lower ranks and by district captains. Contracts with the police union reduced police managers' ability to deploy their officers as they saw fit or to change work rules. Only 10 percent of department personnel were civilians, the lowest proportion of any police agency in the 10 largest cities at the time. Equipment was out of date and often inoperable. Many police buildings were in a state of disrepair.

The task force report also brought to light the positive policing initiatives that individual commanders had been fostering. The report described how these initiatives fit in with a developing national trend toward community policing. Using the report to create a climate for change, Chief Tucker began to formulate a strategy.

One of his first moves was to send command personnel to the Senior Management Institute for Police (SMIP), a three-week management program sponsored by PERF. The purpose of SMIP is to bring police managers together in a classroom setting and provide them with intensive education in the best available management theory and practice. The primary goal of the training is to stimulate thinking about relevant changes that could—and should—be made in the managers' departments.

According to Deputy Commissioner William Bergman, a captain under Tucker, SMIP was among the best training programs the department supplied to its top managers. Bergman felt SMIP "forced the students to think about the future of the agency and the strategies that were instrumental in reaching our goals."

First Deputy Commissioner Tom Seamon felt that Tucker set the foundation for departmentwide adoption of community policing. According to Seamon, some agency administrators felt they were being "brainwashed into believing in community policing." Tucker made a conscious effort to reach beyond the agency's top administrators and train lieutenants and captains, so they would be included in the change process. Upper management did not appreciate this tactic, but it appears that it was key to effecting change in the department. As of 1993, all of the department's top command officers had been middle managers under Tucker, and all had received training at SMIP.

During his tenure, Tucker implemented a number of departmental changes. He directed the development of a mission statement that set the department's sights outward and said the department would become more responsive to Philadelphia's many diverse communities. He created the Police Commissioner's Council, a cross-section of prominent civic leaders who met with the commissioner monthly to advise him on issues affecting the community and the department. Tucker had district captains create neighborhood advisory councils, also composed of local civic leaders, to provide citizens with information. To address the demands for a greater police presence, Tucker opened a number of ministations that were the staging points for neighborhood foot patrols. He assigned victim assistance officers to each police district to help victims file complaints, testify in court, obtain compensation, and acquire needed help. Tucker also assigned a crime prevention officer to each district to conduct crime prevention surveys. Additionally, community relations officers were assigned to every district captain to coordinate all district-level and citywide programs aimed at bringing the police and the community together. Finally, Drug Abuse Resistance Education (DARE) personnel were assigned to teach various public and parochial grade school students about the consequences of drug abuse.

Despite the objections of many of the department's top executives, Tucker undertook an experiment in decentralization in the southern division. This experiment was intended to set the stage for departmentwide decentralization by serving as a model for the future. Detective operations were decentralized to the division's inspector, Edward McLaughlin. McLaughlin and his four district captains were given relative autonomy in policing their communities. In an unprecedented move, McLaughlin applied for and won a federal grant to apply a problem-oriented approach to drugs in four beats within his command. Under this program, a number of problem-solving efforts were undertaken, primarily by the special foot patrol officers assigned to the area and the three district specialist officers (for victim assistance, crime prevention and community relations).

Tucker resigned in 1988, before most of his reform efforts could be implemented. His resignation was met with sadness and anger from many of the middle managers who had allied themselves with him as he tried to change the department. But even some of his supporters felt Tucker had not moved quickly enough to decentralize the department and reassign senior officials who obstructed change.

Willie Williams succeeded Tucker as police commissioner, becoming the first African American to hold the job. Immediately after Tucker's resignation, and as Williams was settling into his new position, there was great uncertainty as to whether further changes would be implemented and recent changes rescinded. Of direct concern to some middle managers was whether upper-level managers would take the victim assistance, crime prevention and community relations officers away from district captains. This concern was not unjustified, as senior officials had previously tried to send these officers back to patrol.

Following a period of uncertainty within the department, Williams developed a "five-point plan" for the agency. In four pages, the plan addressed the five points: community policing; narcotics enforcement; career and staff development; technological and planning improvement; and social, legal and economic accountability. The complete section on community policing read:

> Community policing is a process of solving problems: community problems about crime and disorder. It is a central theme to be emphasized in this department. We will expand and elaborate on programs that solve community problems, and that address quality-of-life issues in neighborhoods.
>
> Ministations help to stabilize neighborhoods, and we will continue to support their development with the active assistance of residents. Victim assistance, crime prevention and community relations officers are not luxuries in this department. They form an alternative response to citizen and community problems, and they are an active ingredient in any scheme for community policing—we will not abandon these functions.
>
> Police officers working the sector cars, the emergency patrol wagon or walking the foot beat are also important to community policing programs. They must be actively involved because community policing is not a specialty in this department—it is our way of providing service throughout the community.
>
> Community policing also stresses officer, supervisor and commander accountability to the clients of our service—the citizens of Philadelphia. All of our efforts should be directed to providing a responsive service to Philadelphia's many and varied communities. Because of the differences that exist across communities, this policing strategy will take many forms. What works in one section of the City may not in another. What is recognized, however, is that police personnel, in conjunction with citizens, will identify community problems, analyze their causes and methods to resolve them, and implement programs to reduce these problems. Problem solving is a key to this initiative and a charge to all department personnel.

Williams carried on with many of the changes Tucker implemented. The specialist officers assigned to captains and the ministations were retained. A career development program for middle managers was created. And the push toward decentralization continued. (By the time Williams was asked to become police chief in Los Angeles in 1992, the entire department had been decentralized.) Many department command officers felt Williams' support of community policing propelled him into national prominence and led to his appointment to the Los Angeles position.

Richard Neal, another African American from within the department's ranks, was appointed commissioner when Williams went to Los Angeles. Neal saw his role in the implementation process as one of opening the department to the public. As a result, Neal depended heavily on advisory groups and citizens to receive feedback about the department's attitude, image and actions.

The citizens groups provided written recommendations that Neal's office reviewed. For example, the Citizens' Advisory Group expressed concerns about some department members' racial attitudes. As a result of citizen input on this topic, Neal had the entire department undergo cultural awareness training.

Neal stated that community policing is a "top down" philosophy that starts with an agency's lead administrator. In Philadelphia, it initially involved identifying the people who would play a role in making the changes and putting those people into place. The final stage of community policing implementation, which Neal was undertaking, involved disseminating information to the lower ranks about community policing and how it helps officers do their jobs. Neal believed that most of the officers in the department understood the community policing philosophy, and that the community policing implementation process was about 80 percent complete.

Neal said his commitment to community policing was conveyed in all documents distributed within the department and throughout the community. He also believed that the importance of community policing was stressed at all organizational forums, from the academy to roll-call briefings.

Neal claimed that community policing needed to be "injected into all facets of the organization." Neal felt that the following initiatives were vital to the success of the department's community policing efforts:

- a McGruff program at local schools;

- a Police Explorer program that was reinstituted;

- the department's decentralization effort, which included decentralizing narcotics enforcement;

- the Victim Assistance Program, which was expanded to the entire city;

- the abandoned vehicle officers, who were assigned to each district;

- the community policing training, which was provided yearly to each officer, satisfying Pennsylvania's Municipal Police Officer Act;

- the monthly district workshops, attended by community members, at which community policing topics were discussed; and

- the 32 ministations that were opened throughout Philadelphia.

Since 1976, Neal has kept abreast of community policing issues, primarily through the publications and activities of the National Organization of Black Law Enforcement Executives (NOBLE). A longtime member of NOBLE, Neal said his organization provided him with important insights into community policing.

Neal claimed to have received a lot of support from government officials, the community and the police union in his quest to implement community policing. Neal felt the future of community policing in Philadelphia rested on continuous improvement of the concepts, increased involvement of the public, and continuous cooperation between the police and the community.

COMMUNITY POLICING AT WORK

Although community policing in Philadelphia took a number of forms, many in the police department and the community felt captains were the most visible and recognizable manifestation of the initiative. Although captains had been prominent players in the past, their role was enhanced by the move to decentralize department services.[1]

Captains were particularly enthusiastic about their role. A former captain of the 35th District related that his time as a district captain under the community policing concept was "the best two years of my career." The 35th District

---

1. One longtime observer of the Philadelphia Police Department thought the current emphasis on district captains and community groups was a throwback to the department's operational structure in the 1950s and 1960s.

had the first Police District Advisory Council (PDAC) and was one of the first areas involved in problem-oriented policing. Cliff Barcliff, a former captain[2] in the 7th District, which is the largest geographical district in Philadelphia, defined community policing as "pride of place." Barcliff's philosophy of community policing involved taking the time and making the effort to train personnel in this style of policing. He estimated that it took two years to provide officers in his district with a solid understanding of the community policing philosophy. In late 1992, to educate his lieutenants and sergeants, he developed a supervisors' roundtable to discuss and plan the implementation of community policing. To aid in these discussions, he put together a set of readings—reprints of National Institute of Justice pieces and articles from the *FBI Law Enforcement Bulletin* and *Governing Magazine*. Capt. Frank Pryor said most captains in the agency understood community policing and flexibly applied the principles of this philosophy to their job assignments. Twelfth District Capt. Ed Cleary felt that a good community policing program starts with the community's involvement, and that the captain is responsible for ensuring that the department is in the right position to use problem solving, if it is to make a positive impact on the community. It was generally agreed that the captains appreciated staying involved in the community policing programs, which for them meant keeping in contact with their constituents.

The police district advisory councils, created in 1986, were a major constituency for district captains. Tucker said the PDACs were a major departure from the way the agency had traditionally delivered police service. It was thought that PDACs would become a cornerstone of the department's community policing initiatives. The PDACs would include community leaders in the command-level planning process and create a true partnership between the department and citizens by providing a regular forum for interaction.

To assist the captain, each district had a group of officers who were assigned to a community policing team, or the "five squad."[3] The five squad was a group of officers who worked specific assignments. In the 6th District, for example, the five squad consisted of the following positions:

Community relations officer. The community relations officer was the district's primary contact for nonemergency matters of general concern to community members. This officer coordinated PDAC meetings, other community meetings and school programs.

Crime prevention officer. The crime prevention officer worked with individuals and businesses to prevent crime and minimize its effects. This officer conducted security surveys of residences and businesses and suggested ways to prevent burglary and improve safety. In the 6th District, this officer also served as the youth aid panel coordinator and organized crime prevention programs.

Victim assistance officer. The victim assistance officer helped victims of violent crimes by, for example, obtaining medical assistance and recovering payment for hospital bills.

Abandoned vehicle officer. The abandoned vehicle officer was responsible for ensuring that abandoned vehicles were removed.

Sanitation officer. The sanitation officer was responsible for handling complaints about trash and littering, improper disposal and dumpster usage. This officer was concerned with curtailing the dumping of household or business trash at public litter barrels and with seeing that trash was placed curbside only on the proper collection days.

Each of these specialist officers worked directly under a sergeant. They seemed to have an immense impact on citizens' understanding of community policing, as they worked on a coordinated basis with citizens. Officers assigned to this squad were selected based on their interpersonal skills and demonstrated abilities to work with limited

---

2. He retired from the department shortly after the site study was completed and became the police chief in another Pennsylvania city.

3. The term *five squad* originated with another group of officers whom captains had at their disposal. To compensate for the four-platoon shift schedule that deployed officers equally around the clock, a squad of officers was assigned to the captain to be used as needed to address pressing problems. Though this particular group no longer exists, the name was attached to the specialist officers assigned to captains.

supervision. While regular patrol officers were responsive to radio calls and crises, the five squad was the one group that was responsive to the captain.

Captains felt community policing in Philadelphia did not significantly involve personnel below their rank. One high-ranking official said, "Captains of the districts have become extremely powerful because of community policing, and at times, this causes them to become reluctant to allow lower ranks to develop within this philosophy." The official went on to say that district captains have become "political leaders" whom community members love. The community's high demands on captains' time force them to work increasingly harder to please the citizens and leaves them less time to develop staff. Lieutenants and sergeants played minimal roles in day-to-day community policing operations. This concerned a number of senior officials and was often mentioned as something that needed further attention. Several captains said the biggest challenge in community policing was getting the officers on the street more involved. There was widespread agreement that community policing in Philadelphia would be incomplete until the officers on the street consistently played a role.

An exception to captains' dominant role in community policing was found in the Center City District. A lieutenant headed this district, which includes the core downtown businesses. Merchants in this district paid an extra tax for increased sanitation services and uniformed civilian aides, who assisted shoppers, tourists and others who frequented the downtown area. The city added extra police to patrol this area, and they were based out of a special station in the heart of downtown.

Police department members did not unanimously support community policing. Two senior officers assigned to patrol related that the majority of officers generally did not like community policing. They felt the agency did not have enough officers to support such a program. Some officers felt the captain or the special officers assigned to him or her should be responsible for coordinating community policing activities. Several officers suggested that community policing be taught initially to officers in the academy, which would allow them to contribute to the effort as soon as they were hired.

Some officers also said that older officers have difficulty accepting this philosophy and that "50 percent of the officers on the street understand it, but only 1 percent accept it, and that's stretching it." It was difficult to differentiate skepticism about community policing from officers' other concerns: inoperable equipment, defective vehicles, run-down buildings, and lack of pay increases. These concerns may have increased officers' reluctance to accept community policing. One officer mentioned that community members have traditionally been anti-police. The officer further related that "it's not natural to want to get along and have a partnership with the community when traditionally you haven't had to."

Several agency members felt community policing was not the most accurate description of the department's current philosophy, which one captain described as just "doing good policing." One ranking administrator felt the term *community policing* led officers to believe it was a special program associated with a special unit.

COMMUNITY POLICING AND RACE

Although department members seldom discussed race unless directly addressed, concerns about race were evident throughout Philadelphia. Community policing had begun in response to an incident with strong racial overtones. Affirmative action and racial inequity issues were just below the surface during any discussion of promotions with department personnel.

Deputy Commissioner Bergman, the operations south commander, said that "community policing enhances racial harmony and has opened the police department up to the minority community." Bergman further stated that "community policing has allowed minority groups to be a part of the strategic plan for the police department, and that is definitely a first." Bergman felt the policies and procedures practiced under community policing helped the community in developing leaders. This was demonstrated by the existence of citizens groups and the active roles citizens took when working with the police department.

Deputy Commissioner McLaughlin, the operations north commander, said: "Part of community policing is teaching the community how to use the resources of the department. For so long, many segments of our communities, especially the minority communities, didn't understand how to use the department's resources." McLaughlin felt community policing provided an avenue for every citizen to actively work with the department.

Barbara Daniels, an African-American resident of the 6th District, felt community policing helped the agency to work more closely with minority communities. Daniels stated that "10 years ago, the relationship between the Philadelphia Police Department and minority communities was very controversial." Daniels said that African Americans saw police as the enemy, and that one of the contributing factors to this image was the lack of communication between the police and the community.

Daniels felt that, under the leadership of her district captain, "there is an effort on the part of the police to get the residents more involved, and an increased attempt to break down the racial barriers that exist between law enforcement and the minority communities." Daniels felt this effort was evidenced by the department's increased communication efforts.

However, Daniels still felt that a segment of the African-American community remained skeptical about the police's true motives in working with the community. She thought a continuing effort would be required on the part of the department to end racial strife and work toward a better quality of life for all citizens. Daniels, a school community coordinator for the Philadelphia School District, felt community policing was necessary if today's minority youths were ever to respect the police.

The 6th District was working closely with local schools to ensure that youths understood that the police really do care about them. The 6th District adopted the local high school; every month, two high school students were invited to attend the police-sponsored advisory meetings. Daniels felt programs such as those helped to change the negative image of the department and let the community see officers function as "normal" human beings.

Daniels also applauded the ministation in her district, which she says forced the officers who work there to stay in touch with the community. She felt proactive police programs were a requirement if minority residents were to feel the police department really cared about their having a better quality of life.

Anna Jung, a Chinese-American resident and member of the Police Advisory Board for the 6th District, felt the relationship between the police and minority communities had greatly improved over the past 10 years. She said, "Community policing has definitely helped the image of the Philadelphia Police Department." Jung, a 10-year resident of the community, said that, in the past, the perception of the police department was not very good, and citizens were very disappointed with the agency.

Jung said the department's image has been changed due to "the cooperative working relationship that we have with the officers on a daily basis." Jung related that the community she lives in is multiracial and multiethnic, and that she believes the only way you can do good policing in such a neighborhood is to have continuous open communication between the police and the community.

THE FUTURE OF COMMUNITY POLICING IN PHILADELPHIA

"Community policing is a philosophy of service delivery; within the philosophy is problem solving, and this service delivery is currently in the fifth year of a 10-year plan," stated McLaughlin. The feelings about community policing in the Philadelphia Police Department are those of optimism, confusion, apprehension, necessity, and enthusiasm. At the street level, officers interviewed who were not part of a five squad had little understanding of what community policing was about. They had difficulty articulating a definition of the concept and did not see how it fit into their job. When asked about training received, one officer, who supported community policing, could remember participating only in sensitivity, diversity and ethnic training.

Other officers saw community policing as a public relations stunt that thwarted their ability to fight crime. Department leaders were well aware that personnel below the rank of captain have not been consistently engaged in community policing, and it appeared that educating lieutenants, sergeants and officers would be a lengthy process. Nevertheless, as gauged by how the public viewed the police, community policing may have improved relations between the police and citizens.

Throughout the organization, there was agreement that community policing can benefit both the agency and the community. Bergman said that Philadelphia, with its 1.6 million residents, is a city of neighborhoods that are divided along racial and ethnic lines, which allows for community policing to be naturally implemented. He went on to explain that the local politicians grew up in Philadelphia and understand the importance of community-based policing efforts. The consensus among department administrators was that community policing demands that officers work smarter, be innovative and do their jobs properly. Bergman felt that for community policing to be a dynamic program for the agency in the 1990s and beyond, personnel would need to understand that "it's a complete attitude change in the way that customers are treated."

Department captains felt that for the entire agency to practice community policing, all officers would have to be trained in it. Commissioner Neal claimed that his citizens groups helped the department to identify cultural awareness training as a very important aspect of community policing. At the completion of the cultural awareness training, the department planned to go back to the community and ask for an overall assessment of the program. This training will be one of the key components for ensuring that community policing survives over the next few years.

Many department personnel felt community policing brought key people from all neighborhoods together through involvement in city groups. It was also related on numerous occasions that community policing has helped police defuse racial situations quicker than they could in the past, due to enhanced racial harmony. The future of community policing in the Philadelphia Police Department will depend on key groups' feeling they are in a partnership with the agency.

A police officer assigned to the 6th District said: "Community policing is a necessity for the minority communities and the Philadelphia Police Department. I don't care what anyone says. I think this concept assisted us during the uprisings after the Rodney King trial." He added: "It may be unfair to relate this, but I looked at the riots that occurred around the country, and I felt that this was a mechanism for the minority communities to openly state that they demand equal and fair treatment by law enforcement. And I think that's what an ideal community policing program provides—fair and equal law enforcement for all citizens."

Community-Oriented Problem Solving in Santa Barbara, Calif.

by George Barrett

INTRODUCTION

Standing at well over 6 feet tall and weighing in at close to 250 pounds, Richard A. Breza is a large and commanding figure. As the chief of the Santa Barbara, Calif., Police Department, however, Breza has an impact that more than supersedes his size. He is a man of vision, committed to effective leadership of the agency and endowed with the political savvy to put his ideas into action.

His vision of policing has taken the shape of community-oriented problem solving, or COPS, although it is difficult to determine whether this approach is more akin to generic community policing and problem-solving principles or more the result of Breza's influence by philosophical mentor Tom Peters, author of *In Search of Excellence*. This book advocated such bold new management concepts as risk-taking at all organizational levels, orientation toward the future, management contracts, and team approaches to decision-making. Breza's commitment to the Peters style is evident throughout the agency, from the personnel's language and stated ambitions to the framed posters on the walls, carrying such maxims as "Aim High." Because of Breza's commitment to the concept, COPS has become a policing philosophy for the Santa Barbara Police Department, an approach that is well-understood and articulated by personnel throughout the agency, from dispatchers to line officers to investigations staff. And although the path to his community policing goals is not complete, the story of its construction provides a useful blueprint for other police agencies.

THE CITY OF SANTA BARBARA

Santa Barbara is a crescent-shaped city nestled along California's west coast. A mountain ridge to the north of the city forms a protective wall. Area residents have enjoyed a moderate climate and comfortable living conditions since before the city was established as a Franciscan outpost in the late 18th century.

Santa Barbara's growth has been steady and deliberate. In part because of its distance from Los Angeles, 100 miles to the south, and San Francisco, 330 miles to the north, the city has been spared the rapid increase in industry and suburban development that has taxed other regions of the state. This stability allowed a comfortable upper class to evolve by the early 20th century. A small downtown business district remains very much as it appeared in the 1920s. Residential growth has moved slowly toward the mountain ridge to the north and along the coastal plain to the east and west.

Santa Barbara has a reputation for affluence—the median price for a house is $300,000—but today there is another side to the story. Per capita income in the city is actually over 5 percent below the state's average. To ensure a steady revenue source, the city has promoted tourism as a major industry. However, the drought that plagued California for over five years, coupled with the generally high cost of living, has limited the number of tourists visiting the city over the past two years.

Santa Barbara's population has steadily increased since 1960—growing 46 percent overall since 1960, and 15 percent in the decade from 1980 to 1990. Census date (see table 1) reflect this steady growth.

Table 1
Santa Barbara Population, by Decade

Year		Population
1960		58,768
1970		70,215
1980		74,414
1990		85,571
2000	(projected)	96,731

Perhaps the most important dimension of Santa Barbara's growth is the rise in the city's Hispanic population. Hispanics—most of Mexican descent—make up 30 percent of the population. Whites make up 61 percent of the population, and Asians, American Indians and blacks constitute the rest.

Santa Barbara's growing Hispanic population has been recognized as an important factor in political decisions, social programs, budget planning, and staffing. It is widely believed that more Hispanics are living in Santa Barbara than the census data reveal—perhaps another 5,000 to 10,000 undocumented Mexican immigrants. The city also has a large homeless community of up to 2,000.

The young and growing Hispanic population has created a demand for Santa Barbara (and other California cities) to make major changes in providing education, social services, law enforcement, housing, and economic planning. Competing interests and economic woes have produced profound changes in resource allocation. Initiatives for reduced state taxes and more state programs have resulted in counties' and cities' being assigned an increased share of the responsibility for government, necessitating creative programs, efficient government and increased private-sector involvement.

SANTA BARBARA CITY ADMINISTRATION

Breza and the Santa Barbara Police Department have had a receptive environment in which to implement change, partially because of strong support from the city administrator's office. Richard D. Thomas has been the city administrator for the past 16 years.

Santa Barbara adopted the council-mayor-city administrator form of government in 1967. The current political structure seems to serve the interests of the city's business community and status quo politicians. But the political winds in Santa Barbara may be changing. In 1990, an attempt was made to change the method of selecting the six-member city council; the measure was narrowly defeated by voters. This attempt to change the council selection process was attributed to efforts among the growing Hispanic community to gain more influence in city government. One of the current council members is Hispanic; he was appointed to fill a vacancy. Despite his heritage, some members of the Hispanic community view him as a member of the existing business community and not as a representative of their views and concerns.

So far, the Hispanic community has been unable to organize into a single recognizable group or to select a leader. Hispanics are most often heard from following an incident involving their community, but seldom are they regarded as a consistent force to be included in administrative decision-making. Jesse Chavarria, a reporter who covers police-related issues for the Santa Barbara daily newspaper, described the situation: "Latinos in Santa Barbara come together on immediate issues that touch them or their families; once the matter is over, they go home." Thus, the Hispanic community's leverage on politicians remains an issue for the future.

In 1992, voters approved a referendum to limit the number of terms council members and the mayor could serve. Thus, at the time of this writing, the city's current mayor planned to leave office upon completion of her third four-year term, and the city administrator planned to retire during 1993. New leadership may point the city in different directions, particularly as the city struggles to come to grips with service demands from the growing Hispanic population.

Breza and City Administrator Thomas seemed to have a collegial relationship, with little political interference from elected officials noticeable to the casual observer. However, it is clear that efforts are made to proactively provide politicians with sufficient information to prevent overt political involvement. The lack of major crimes and the relatively stable crime level in the community in recent years (see table 2) contribute to the political equilibrium that seems to exist.

Table 2
Santa Barbara Reported Crimes, by Year

	1990	1991	1992	Percentage Increase
Murder	5	5	5	0
Rape	27	38	35	30
Robbery	131	151	163	24
Assault	471	480	489	4
Theft	3,037	3,015	3,382	11

Excerpts from Santa Barbara Police Department, 1990, 1991, 1992
Crime analysis report dated Feb. 17, 1993

Despite the political equilibrium, the city council and administrator have maintained a strong interest in law enforcement over the years. The police department receives the biggest portion of the city's budget funds, and cutbacks have occurred in recent years, notably for capital expenditures. Nonetheless, among other city employees, the police department has a reputation as a "sacred cow" at budget time.

The council, however, has been concerned about the direction of policing. In fact, Breza was specifically selected as chief as an intentional contrast to the agency's previous chiefs. According to Thomas, previous chiefs had preferred to maintain a "distant relationship" with the community. The city tried to introduce innovation to the department in 1980 by hiring an "outside" chief. A controversial incident resulted in his leaving the department; his successor was promoted from within the agency in 1982. His administration was characterized as a caretaker administration for the four years before Breza was selected.

THE SANTA BARBARA POLICE DEPARTMENT

The Santa Barbara Police Department is a relatively specialized municipal agency. Its 138 sworn officers are divided among three divisions—investigative, operations and administrative—each commanded by a captain. In addition, the department has a deputy chief. In total, this command group constitutes what is known among the officers as "The Third Floor."

The department is housed in a picturesque building that is prominently featured on the department's letterhead and other materials. Known in past years as "The Citadel" because of the historical arm's-length distance between the police and the community, the building provides tight quarters for the department's personnel. Department personnel have state-of-the-art communications and dispatching equipment and late-model, well-maintained squad cars.

The department's sworn personnel are largely well-educated. In a sample of patrol officers, 5 percent had only a high school diploma, while 33 percent had a four-year college degree and an additional 10 percent had graduate-level education.

In recent years, the department has tried to increase minority representation at the patrol level. However, at the time of this writing, the department had no minority or female officers above the rank of sergeant. The department's personnel breakdown was as follows:

	White	Black	Hispanic	Asian	Female
Captain	3	0	0	0	0
Lieutenant	7	0	0	0	0
Sergeant	18	0	2	0	0
Officer II	40	1	12	1	3
Officer	31	2	6	2	4

One problem for the department has been the lack of Spanish-speaking officers on the force; it has not been unusual for officers responding to an incident or call to take a Spanish-speaking secretary or call-taker along to translate. The department was planning to make a Spanish language and culture class available for officers in 1993, and it was to involve an immersion component in Mexico. Personnel are paid a small differential for Spanish language skills.

LEADERSHIP

Breza joined the Santa Barbara Police Department in 1971 and rose through the ranks to captain. He attended the California Police Command College, which he credits with giving him many of the ideas he later implemented.

Breza admits that, as a captain, he was strongly influenced by many of the management concepts Peters discussed. "The staff that I had at the time I became chief never had to take risks; most of them did not feel comfortable with this idea. As they left [the agency], I was able to promote officers who could work in this new environment," he said. Breza's staff now bears the mark of his influence: all of the agency's three captains and five lieutenants, as well as 14 of its 19 sergeants, were promoted by Breza to their current positions and were required to demonstrate knowledge of community policing as part of the promotional process. Among senior command staff, only the deputy chief is a holdover from previous administrations.

In his early years of mid-level management within the department, Breza was frustrated by the lack of interaction between the department and the community. "A lack of interaction stemmed from both the department's traditional methods of policing and the fact that the department was doing its own thing, with no significant involvement from the community," he recalled. The high cost of housing in the county, which forced about 60 percent of the department's personnel to buy homes in other counties and commute to work, also contributed to the lack of interaction. Many of the department's newer officers reportedly felt no tie to Santa Barbara.

Under Breza's command, formal community policing efforts with a problem-solving dimension began in the department in about 1989. Community outreach efforts had begun in 1987. "The goal in community policing is working with the community to reduce the fear of crime," Breza said. Capt. Jeree Johnson described the transition to COPS as a process in which the department changed from the traditional agency it was before Breza took over to one that was involved in community policing. "The community policing idea was primarily a public relations concept that was largely driven at the time in Santa Barbara by issues involving the homeless. The department had become more image-conscious and, at the same time, under Chief Breza, was becoming more active in social and community issues," said Johnson.

But the move to community policing and problem solving was also motivated by efforts to increase the department's efficiency. "Officers were being called to the same locations four to six times in a night; they were handling calls for service all over the city, but not accomplishing anything," said Breza. "The problems were not being addressed, so I decided that we should put one beat coordinator on each of our six beats. The old method of arresting someone to solve the problem was not working." For Breza, the beat coordinator approach would allow police interaction with the community to be structured. After visits to nearby Oxnard, Calif., and extensive reading and investigation, his staff recommended that the department establish a beat coordinator position as a method to address community problems.

OPERATIONALIZATION OF COPS

A cadre of specialist officers was assembled to supplement patrol officers. Santa Barbara is organized into six geographical beats. Patrol officers from the three watches are assigned to each beat and have primary responsibility for calls for service and patrol-related activity, as well as for involvement in addressing community problems.

Beat coordinators were selected in a competitive process and formally assigned to each of the six beats to coordinate problem-solving efforts, particularly working with the community and accessing other resources. When possible, beat coordinators work with patrol officers, using directed patrol and community resources to address specific problems. Beat coordinators routinely handle calls for service for a portion of their daily shift—usually three hours out of 10. This call-handling responsibility ensures that the specialists do not become isolated from patrol concerns. Similarly, the department placed the beat coordinators with the patrol (operations) division to avoid the isolation problem.

Beat coordinators attend many community meetings and meet with key people on their beat at least once a week. They serve as a contact when residents and other agency officials have a problem or concern. They routinely solicit community input, occasionally using community surveys to develop a better understanding of specific problems. In addition, they make themselves available to citizens, routinely distributing cards with their name and phone number.

Much of the beat coordinator's job is to coordinate resources. "I see myself as a resource and idea man," explained Officer Kim Fryslie, one of the department's six beat coordinators. "Getting the problem solved often involves me knowing who to call outside the department. Having a good relationship means I can get things accomplished without a lot of delays."

One of the most demanding neighborhood problems involved garbage that needed to be collected. Before COPS, the city's best efforts simply involved police officers' issuing parking tickets to clear the streets in a neighborhood. The public works department would then clean the pavement with street sweepers.

Fryslie began with a neighborhood survey that provided advance notice that the city would be using Operation Clean Sweep in a neighborhood. The city would clean the neighborhood's streets, and the parks department would trim trees and shrubs. A dumpster would be provided to give residents the opportunity to clean up their yards and houses. During the day, the police department would host a cookout for the residents.

The new effort reduced the number of cars towed from the streets, improved the cleanup's effectiveness, increased participation in cleaning up private property, and improved the police department's image. When Operation Clean Sweep was implemented, it worked well with the city beautification program. One example of how this program has worked is residents' continued effort in one neighborhood to clean up graffiti as it appears.

Another example of the department's focus on collaborating with other agencies is its Crossroads program. Crossroads is a creative multiagency effort to involve youths in eradicating graffiti through the development of murals. The program began as a problem-solving effort to address city graffiti.

To encourage problem solving throughout the department, supervision of beat coordinators was organized under the department's operations lieutenant and sergeant. Sgt. Rich Abney, who was reassigned following the reorganization of several units, currently oversees the beat coordinators. He views his role as that of facilitator for these officers. He manages the record-keeping for the unit, works with the watch supervisors to include them in COPS, and provides training on problem solving to the department. Abney uses a 14-page COPS manual (plus forms) to guide the training of beat coordinators and other personnel. This document outlines key steps for officers to use in addressing community problems. It is a model borrowed largely from the Newport News, Va., Police Department.

The department tracks problem solving using departmental forms; however, this process seems largely informal. Two forms available for documentation are the problem identification interview form, which documents information collected from citizen complaints, and the problem analysis report, which documents initiation, supervisory approval and other information regarding an officer's work. Problem-solving files are not centralized; nor are forms indexed. The watch commanders maintain a directed patrol log to record patrol work directed at problems on the beats. Beat coordinators keep individual files on problems they are addressing, including such information as correspondence, crime analysis reports and the like.

Addressing problems, however, has not been restricted to the beat coordinators. "Although we were using beat coordinators as the focal point of COPS, everyone was expected to do it, not just talk about it," explained one police official.

Patrol officers receive training in community policing and problem solving from both formal and informal sources. Newly hired officers receive training at the academy in subjects that touch on community policing and problem solving. When officers return to the department, they receive several more hours of training from the beat coordinators in problem solving. General training for veteran officers has consisted of

- roll-call training videotapes,

- training bulletins received from the state or from other departments relating to COPS,

- an internal memorandum describing the department's COPS program, and

- one-on-one instruction by beat coordinators.

Officers also attend conferences throughout the state. In addition, they are expected to read on their own about community policing and problem solving. The most effective means of informing patrol officers about COPS has been through their daily contact with the beat coordinators, according to Abney. Beat coordinators attend conferences and receive training in time management, public speaking, public presentations, and cultural awareness.

Training is also supplemented in other ways designed to enhance communication throughout the agency. For example, the department's monthly newsletter features the "Beat Coordinators Corner," written by the administrative sergeant. Communication is enhanced through information sharing. For example, call-takers routinely attend briefings for each patrol shift to exchange information about community problems. Similarly, efforts have been made to integrate community-based problem solving into every part of the department. Even the investigations division has gotten involved in problem solving.

Lt. David McCoy, watch commander on the swing shift, believes patrol officers do engage in addressing problems. He cited an example in which a city night spot was creating problems in the surrounding neighborhood, primarily because patrons were leaving the tavern and urinating outside. An officer realized that the problem, in part, was due to the tavern's having only one restroom. He had several portable restrooms put alongside the tavern, thereby providing patrons with additional facilities. This substantially reduced the number of complaints neighbors made about the tavern.

Beat coordinators routinely assist patrol officers in addressing problems. For example, Officer Jerry McBeth, an 11-year veteran of the department, was assigned to the swing shift. He thought the COPS program simply entailed using community resources to solve problems. He learned about the COPS program by working with one of the beat coordinators, "Skip" Bond. McBeth and Bond worked to reduce loitering in one of the city parks, a problem that had prompted complaints. They used directed patrol to move the loiterers out of the park and thus reduce complaints. Making traffic stops around the park was also effective in discouraging loitering.

Watch commanders receive a monthly summary of beat coordinators' problem-solving efforts. This is one of the primary means for informing officers about the department's progress. Beat coordinators also attend roll call, and, at the time of this writing, the department had recently put up "beat boards," white boards in the briefing room on which beat coordinators posted information such as calls-for-service summaries and queries about individual problems being addressed.

As a watch commander, Lt. Charlie Calkins views his role "as a balancing act, attempting to handle calls for service and COPS. COPS is not a comfortable component in the department, but I prefer to handle it, rather than having it assigned [to me from] outside the operations unit," he said.

The extent to which the department's focus on community policing and problem solving has overcome traditional resistance is unclear. Despite the department's perceived success in implementing COPS, "the patrol force is completely incident-driven, and the officers still regard their primary responsibility as responding quickly to runs," said Calkins.

Despite efforts to involve patrol officers in addressing problems, the department's major obstacle is the lack of beat integrity. According to Capt. Edward Aasted, operations commander, officers at best spend 60 percent of their time on the beat; they spend the other 40 percent driving across the city, responding to calls. One study showed that each officer was encumbered for 70 percent of his or her watch (SBPD Operations Division Audit, March 1993). The department has struggled with an increasing call load: in 1971, there were 38,000 calls for service; in 1992, there were 125,000 calls for service—a 229 percent increase. Nonetheless, Aasted hopes beat officers can engage in some problem solving during their shifts; if they cannot handle problems they identify or if they are too busy on calls, they can work with the beat coordinator to address the problems.

Despite being busy on calls, at least some police officers engage in problem solving. New beat coordinators are selected largely on the basis of their participation in problem solving as patrol officers. For example, Officer Mike Aspland was selected in early 1993 as a beat coordinator. Aspland, who for the previous three years was a member of the tactical patrol force, identified and addressed the labor line problem at 600 Anacapa St. Competing to get work from prospective employers, people often jumped uninvited into the back of pickup trucks stopped at traffic signals, disrupting the traffic flow. The workers also were creating concern at a day care center across from the labor line, because they flowed into the center's parking lot. With input from other personnel, officers decided to move the labor line to another location several blocks away, out of the heart of the city. Moving the group would minimize disruptions and reduce public concern.

Aspland used problem solving to address the labor line problem. During the oral interview for the beat coordinator position, Aspland described his experiences as evidence of his work in addressing community problems. Competition for the specialty beat coordinator assignments is demanding—candidates are expected to both understand problem solving and demonstrate how they have applied the concept.

In addition to the rigorous selection process, the COPS initiative is supported through the Problem Analysis Advisory Committee. This group occasionally meets on an ad hoc basis, primarily to support officers' problem-solving efforts. The group may assist with brainstorming, identifying organizations with which to collaborate, or facilitating officers' problem-solving efforts in other ways.

CHANGING THE ORGANIZATION

Programmatic efforts related to the COPS initiative have not been segregated from the rest of the department. Because community policing and problem solving are viewed as an organizational strategy and philosophy rather than a program, the department has used a variety of means, including various administrative approaches, to meet its objectives and make its chief's vision a reality. The department has intentionally not used a strategic planning process to chart its direction, preferring the flexibility of a less structured approach. However, such methods as selection and training, promotion and performance review systems, and career development or rotation plans have been designed to reinforce the primacy of community policing and problem solving as the means by which police officers do their jobs. For example, the department has selected police recruits who are consistent with its goals. The chief can accept or reject the top candidates for vacant positions during the final interview. During this process, he emphasizes the department's approach to community service and problem solving. Some candidates are rejected because of a discernable lack of understanding of the community.

Proposed Entry-Level Oral Board Questions

- What do you know about the City of Santa Barbara's ethnic makeup, crime rate and cost of living, as well as our method of policing?

- Do you understand the Santa Barbara Police Department is in partnership with the community to solve crime-related problems as well as community problems?

- Solving problems oftentimes involves some risk-taking. Give us some examples of problems that you have solved and the associated risk that you have taken.

Proposed questions, Dec. 7, 1991

"The type of people we're looking for has changed [over the years]," said the department's training sergeant. He acknowledged that the agency has tried to get local candidates "because they have a vested interest in the community" consistent with the department's.

Once selected, new officers attend a pre-academy training session. They are given an overview of the police department, and the importance of community service and problem solving is emphasized. Capt. Greg Stock said that "with the chief's blessing, they go [to the academy] with the attitude that we want them to be successful." The department contracts with other agencies for spots in appropriate training academies. The last academy that was used, at the San Bernardino County, Calif., Sheriff's Department, lasted 22 weeks. The fourth week of training included the following:

- one hour on community service

- one hour on community attitudes

- one hour on citizens' evaluation of law enforcement

- three hours on interpersonal communications

- 13 hours on cultural awareness

Training center course schedule
San Bernardino County Sheriff's Department

Upon returning from the 22-week academy, new officers attend a three-day training program that includes a two-hour explanation of COPS. They then are assigned to a field training officer (FTO). "The FTOs are expected to demonstrate problem solving and reinforce that this is the way we do business in Santa Barbara," explained one officer. The sergeant who supervises the beat coordinators is tasked with training FTOs in problem-solving techniques and procedures, as well as maintaining close contact with FTOs to ensure consistency in the training of new recruits.

Advancement within the department and assignment to specialized positions often depend on officers' understanding of COPS principles and ability to describe how they apply the problem-solving process to their work. New officer evaluation forms were scheduled to be in place in 1993 to measure officers' understanding of COPS and document their involvement in problem solving.

Problem-solving techniques are used throughout the department. For example, a narcotics sergeant and his team of detectives were preparing to serve a drug search warrant. In the past, it would have taken an hour to do so. Using the COPS approach, the narcotics officers had housing and code enforcement inspectors accompany them as part of the process. Once the narcotics officers served the warrant, arrested the suspects and seized the drugs, the other agency inspectors cited the property owner for a long list of violations and boarded up the property. This process lasted more than four hours, but it effectively removed a drug location from the neighborhood.

In addition to providing operational support for its COPS initiative, the department demonstrates its commitment to COPS in its value statement, motto and mission statement. The agency's motto is "Dedicated to Serve," and its mission statement incorporates the following: "We are dedicated to high-quality community-oriented police service. . . . We believe in collaborative problem solving with concerned citizens to identify ways of dealing with neighborhood problems, issues and activities . . ."

To promote pride and city identification, the department also changed the design of its badge and its patch, from one common to the state to one unique to Santa Barbara. The department's logo uses the word "POLICE," spelling out the leading terms in the department's value statement: **P**ride, **O**bjectivity, **L**eadership, **I**ntegrity, **C**ommitment, and **E**xcellence.

The department's career rotation plan met with some resistance upon initiation. The plan stipulated that officers in specialist positions be reassigned every three years. Officers in specialist positions, including beat coordinators, receive salary differentials. An assignment to a specialist position does not ensure that an officer will keep that position, classified as "Officer II." Thus, it is likely that the selection process for these assignments will remain highly competitive.

Clearly, the career development plan serves several different purposes, such as allowing personnel to take on other responsibilities within the agency, including those of beat coordinators. In the long run, such exposure will provide most personnel with a deeper understanding of what the beat coordinators do in addressing community problems. The career development plan also changed the historical path to promotion within the department from the detective division to a variety of other assignments.

Officer Bill Grzybowski, a veteran narcotics officer, was involuntarily rotated to second watch in patrol as part of the career development plan. Despite his concerns, Grzybowski has been able to apply his knowledge of narcotics in combating drug dealing on his beat. He realized a large drug operation was taking place at a house in the Hispanic community on his beat. He arranged to work in plainclothes with two other officers the following night. They set up rooftop surveillance on the location and made several arrests. While watching the drug house, Grzybowski noticed there were prostitutes in the area. He arranged to conduct a similar surveillance directed at the prostitution.

On another night, Grzybowski stood on a corner in the city's downtown area and pointed out four heroin dealers standing across the street. He had noticed them while driving through the area, parked his car and stood across the street in an effort to stop their drug sales. This sent a message to the dealers that he knew who they were and what they were doing, and that it would not be tolerated.

The increased communication and exposure related to career development do not stop with line officers; supervisors have bought into the concept as well. For example, Lt. Calkins, a 25-year veteran of the department, rotated to the day shift to work as the day watch commander. Calkins had worked on the night shift for several years, but had decided to ask for the day work assignment because he wanted to get more involved with the COPS program. Calkins viewed the patrol force, particularly the night shift, as being "out of the loop on COPS." The department for years had stressed problem solving by beat coordinators, but it had placed little emphasis on patrol-level problem solving. Calkins planned to rotate to the swing or mid watch in two or three months to get a broader view of the department and to pass on some of the ideas he had about policing and problem solving. Calkins' interest in changing shifts and learning more serves to illustrate the career-oriented environment the department has nurtured.

Other departmental efforts to support COPS are not programmatic. For example, risk-taking is considered to be "breaking with tradition and putting your reputation on the line—and it starts at the top," explained one sergeant. Breza has encouraged officers to develop innovative responses to community problems. Such responses are sometimes perceived as risky based on their potential for failure. Nonetheless, officers have accepted risk-taking as part of "doing business," with the assurance that they will have the department's support, according to the chief and others at the agency.

For example, one recurring problem in Santa Barbara has been Hispanic teenagers' and young adults' cruising in cars called "low riders" in the city's central area. To address the problem and create a positive image, several officers suggested that the department change an out-of-service police car into a legal version of a low rider. The low-riding police car, known as the "Cruiser," retained police equipment and markings, with the addition of a custom paint finish of two murals: one of the local mission, and one of RoboCop, the robotlike police officer popularized in two movies.

The Cruiser proved controversial both inside and outside the department. Many officers criticized it as a waste of time and money; many residents viewed it as an insult to the Hispanic community. Nonetheless, the Cruiser earned department managers' support and, after its first six months in operation, proved to be popular in the community.

Some patrol officers have also begun problem-solving efforts that were somewhat risky. Neil Sharpe, an 18-year veteran of the department, and Frank Mannix, an officer with five years' experience, researched and proposed a serious habitual offender (SHO) program for juvenile offenders. The SHO program, modeled after a 1986 Justice Department study, involved tracking habitual serious juvenile offenders through the criminal justice system. A juvenile, once identified and classified as an SHO, would receive more consistent and punitive treatment if arrested.

While working on a patrol shift, officers Sharpe and Mannix received approval to research the concept and began collecting information from other agencies to refine the idea for their community. From April until December 1992, they worked closely with the school system, juvenile prosecutors and juvenile court system to develop the actual model to be implemented. While working on the SHO effort, both officers remained in the patrol division, actively handling a workload of calls for service.

The SHO idea became a subject of concern in the Hispanic community, which accused the department of labeling their children and of being culturally biased in applying the program. These concerns necessitated the department's conducting a series of presentations to explain the program and develop support. Despite community concerns, the chief and other police managers have supported the officers throughout the rocky implementation process.

COLLATERAL INITIATIVES

The department has developed and maintained a number of collateral initiatives that helped to institutionalize COPS. For example, the department designed and launched a citizens academy in 1991 to familiarize citizens with policing and involve them in some department activities. Selected community members attended training sessions once a week for four months. The academy has a well-developed curriculum that includes an evening ride-along with a patrol officer.

Annett Carrell, who headed the citizens academy alumni group, explained: "We were targeted [to attend] as people active and visible in the town. We represented those people who had a 'mouth.'. . . [T]he academy increased citizens' awareness of police. Suddenly policemen are something else than just catchers [of criminals]." It is clear that political benefits may result from the citizens academy if the program enhances appreciation of the police among the city's elite. Those who have been selected to attend the citizens academy include a leader in the black community, local reporters and others.

The department's community outreach effort has included the use of "trading cards" (similar to baseball cards) that illustrate individual members of different units. The tactical patrol force, crime prevention unit staff, beat coordinators, SWAT, canine unit staff, and other personnel are featured in photographs on the cards. On the back of each card is basic information about the unit, including its officers' names and its mission. These cards have been popular with community youths and have helped officers make positive community contacts.

In addition to the beat coordinators, the department uses personnel from a number of other units to address community problems. The tactical patrol force uses bicycle patrol, foot patrol and plainclothes officers to target problems in Santa Barbara's downtown area. The traffic unit uses the problem-solving approach as part of the traffic-oriented problem solving (TOPS) program, designed to impact the city's high-accident areas. TOPS involves using both directed enforcement and engineering changes to reduce the number and severity of accidents. Additional efforts closely related to COPS include the department's participation in Neighborhood Watch and Explorer Post and its use of a community relations officer and senior volunteer program.

CONCLUSIONS

Despite the emphasis on problem solving in Santa Barbara, the police department has not lessened its focus on crime and traditional police performance measures. In a random survey of line personnel, officers ranked number and quality of arrests, technical skills (such as report writing), citizen complaints, and appearance as the most important factors their supervisors used in their evaluations. Involvement with the community, problem solving and ability to relate to citizens were rated at half the level of the traditional performance measures. However, almost 60 percent of these officers felt their involvement with COPS affected their potential for promotion.

Department members quickly admit they have not achieved all of their community policing and problem-solving objectives. Breza's goal is "having COPS implemented departmentwide. It's about 65 percent there; in maybe three years it will be completely in place." He views continued community involvement and collaboration with other agencies as key to the success of COPS.

The COPS initiative is difficult to separate from the many other new programs, directions and ideas the Santa Barbara Police Department uses. The department probably would have used the citizens academy, TOPS, officer trading cards, "Cruiser," and foot patrols regardless of the programmatic development of the beat coordinators' positions. The current police administration's management style has laid the groundwork for the institutionalization of change and a more public approach to police work. For these reasons, the actual COPS program can be distinguished only by the use of beat coordinators and by officers' problem solving, while community policing and problem solving in general are clearly viewed as philosophies and organizational approaches to policing.

At the time of this writing, the department had not formally evaluated the impact of its COPS effort. The lack of a formal implementation plan makes an impact or process evaluation pointless. Measuring the success of the Santa Barbara COPS program is difficult, much as it would be in any community. Police and a limited number of city leaders report that police are more open and accessible, and tout the results of individual problem-solving efforts. The department's efforts are clearly well-intended, and they are well-received by the city administration and a large portion of the community. With an emerging Hispanic population that will gain influence and focus this decade, the department will have to address new issues.

Community Policing in Savannah, Ga.

by Jeff Young

INTRODUCTION

The 1991 mayoral race in Savannah, Ga., was a heated campaign. The incumbent mayor, Democrat John P. Rousakis, had served for over 20 years. Until 1991, he had not faced a serious challenge to his reelection bids. His opponent was an unlikely adversary. Republican Susan Weiner was a former resident of New York and had lived in Savannah for only five years. She was the type of candidate who would not ordinarily get voters' support in this Deep South, traditionally Democratic city.

Crime, especially violent crime, was a major campaign issue. In 1991, violent crime was up by 17 percent over the previous year and had risen by over 66 percent since 1989. The city had experienced a large increase in homicides: there were 59 in 1991, compared with 35 in 1990 and 20 in 1989. Much of the violence was attributed to narcotics.

The media focus on the crime problem was significant during the election period. Crime had been cited as the reason for cancellation of a large convention, which greatly concerned local Chamber of Commerce members. Crime was also a major issue in the city council race.

During the bitter campaign, Weiner contended that the city manager should be replaced along with the mayor. Like Rousakis, the city manager had served for many years, and although the position had civil service protection and was not subject to mayoral action, Weiner's call to "clean house" resonated with local voters.

As November drew near, the campaign grew increasingly heated, generating public interest and focusing attention on the police department. Weiner's focus on violent crime provided an incentive for the incumbent mayor and city manager to increase the police department's effectiveness. The police chief recalled: "The city manager told me to do something creative. Community policing seemed like the best bet because of our [previous] successes [using this approach] in public housing."

In October, the police department officially "flipped a switch" and formally launched its community-oriented policing (COP) and problem-oriented policing (POP) initiatives. However, these responses to the crime problem, aimed at improving police service to the community, did not improve the mayor's chances for reelection. With a large voter turnout of 58 percent, Rousakis lost the general election by 2,698 votes; five new aldermen were also elected.

Despite the election-related focus on crime and police service, the first steps in the process of improving police services were already under way by early 1991. The city manager had commissioned a study, known as the Comprehensive Community Crime Control Strategy, which was completed in August 1991. The stated purpose of the study was to develop a comprehensive set of strategies for addressing the city's crime problem. The 350-page study was an extensive assessment of the city's needs, analyzing the distribution and composition of crime among the various neighborhoods, as well as the social and physical characteristics of those neighborhoods. For example, the study mapped the distribution of poverty, physical deterioration, unemployment, child abuse and neglect, teenage pregnancy, and teenage mothers, along with various crime problems.

Proposed strategies addressed not only crime, but also the conditions that foster it. This study became the foundation for the implementation of COP in the Savannah Police Department.

This new, politically motivated emphasis on community policing was not the first example of the department's efforts to develop a cooperative relationship with the community. The department had several earlier programs that were community-based.

EARLY COMMUNITY-BASED PROGRAMS

The Savannah Police Department had experience with community programs before 1991. In 1987, the department participated in the "Showcase Neighborhood Program," which the city manager established as part of the new Neighborhood Services Program to improve the quality of life in troubled neighborhoods. A variety of sources funded the program, including city, state and federal agencies and private foundations. The police department played a major role in the program by working with residents and other city departments to identify needs and establish community priorities. The program philosophy was that city government was a partner with community residents, not a provider for them. In 1990, Savannah received the City Livability Award from the U.S. Conference of Mayors for this program.

In 1988, the police department established four ministations in the city's most troubled public housing developments. Each station had one officer permanently assigned to provide needed police services and develop community links. These officers established relationships with the area residents, especially youths and the elderly. Ministation officers also served as DARE officers in nearby schools and as Boy Scout leaders. Many of these officers organized and coached recreational sports teams.

Before the ministations were established, criminals controlled these neighborhoods. Lt. James Barnwell, who was in charge of the ministations, recalled that fire and paramedic crews had to have a police escort into and out of the areas when responding to calls for service. Patrol officers did not enter these areas without backup from assisting officers. By 1993, officers walked alone in the developments on foot patrols. Children played freely throughout the area, without fear of getting caught in drug dealers' cross fire. Elderly residents were no longer isolated inside due to fear.

The department made other efforts to interact with the community. The department had experimented with bicycle patrols since 1989. Formal implementation began in 1990, and bicycle patrols were used extensively in the downtown and waterfront areas. As a result of public interest, a horse patrol was established in 1987. The horse patrol was also used mainly in the downtown area. The department was working with the community long before it had a formalized COP program. Previous initiatives were, however, solitary efforts that had no relationship to a department-wide philosophy. These programs are still in operation and are important parts of the department's current community policing program.

THE CITY OF SAVANNAH

Savannah is located in the northeastern corner of Georgia. It is a beautiful coastal city, close to the famous Hilton Head, S.C., resort area. The Spanish moss that cascades from the trees and the numerous rows of magnificent old homes evoke memories of Southern splendor. The city boasts one of the nation's largest urban historic districts. Many narrow streets and public squares are still laid out as originally designed by Georgia's founder, James Oglethorpe. Blocks of reclaimed waterfront warehouses have been converted into shops and restaurants that are now major tourist attractions.

The main industries are manufacturing and transportation (port and airport). While not the largest industry, tourism is the fastest-growing industry in Savannah. About 5.1 million people visit Savannah each year. Tourism generates $580 million annually and 16,000 jobs.

The city's current economic status is promising. While not immune, Savannah was resistant to the last recession due to the diversity of its economic base. While the national average for unemployment increased by 4 percent, Savannah experienced a 2 percent increase. The city had a reputation for being financially sound.

Savannah also has its share of problems. Besides the crime problem in the early 1990s, there have been serious problems with urban blight. Many old Victorian homes stand in decay, providing a visual contrast to those homes that have been restored to their previous grandeur. These blighted areas are also the locations for a significant portion of the city's crimes.

Savannah's corporate boundaries encompass 62.6 square miles. According to the 1990 census, the city has a population of 137,560. This population is 51 percent black, 47 percent white and 2 percent other. These percentages have changed gradually over the past 10 years. In 1980, 49 percent of the population was white, and 48 percent was black. From the 1960s to the mid-1970s, there were a number of civil disorders related to racial tensions, but there has been significantly less racial tension over the past 15 years. Instead, there is a high degree of interaction between the black and white populations. Racial tension was not a dominant issue in the implementation of community-based policing.

Savannah operates under a council-manager form of government. The city council, consisting of the mayor and eight other aldermen, is the governing board. The council appoints the chief executive, the city manager, who serves at the pleasure of the board.

THE CITY MANAGER

City Manager Arthur A. Mendonsa has served in the position since 1962. His office is decorated with numerous awards he and the city have received during his tenure. When he joined the city, Savannah's infrastructure was deteriorated. The personnel director had a fourth-grade education, a fact Mendonsa offered as an example of the quality of the city's management employees. Mendonsa's prior experience included eight years as a planner.

Mendonsa has taken an active role in managing the police department, which accounts for 29 percent of the city's budget. Mendonsa describes his input as making "suggestions" for planning by frequently asking, "What are we trying to accomplish?" Mendonsa's office is about one-half mile from police headquarters, and the police chief frequently made the short trip to meet with him.

THE RESHAPING OF THE SAVANNAH POLICE DEPARTMENT

The Comprehensive Community Crime Control Strategy study is an example of the influence Mendonsa's prior planning experience had on his management style. He gathered staff from the city's police, research and budget, and planning and community development departments to conduct the study. The study made recommendations in five strategy areas. The police strategies called for significant changes in the police department and were implemented immediately (in October 1991). All other strategy recommendations were implemented throughout the next year.

The report recommended that the police department decentralize by distributing command accountability on a geographical basis. Previously, patrol captains were assigned to an eight-hour shift and were responsible for all the crimes committed in the city during that time. All line personnel were deployed from the central station, a historic police barracks built in 1870. Based on the report's recommendation, four precincts were designed that grouped crime problems and service areas into manageable sections. Each of the department's four patrol captains was assigned to one of these geographical zones and was responsible for the police activities in that area on a 24-hour basis. They also had authority to schedule and deploy personnel according to precinct and community needs. Precinct stations were established in each defined area, but only for line personnel.

The report's second recommendation was that the department deploy manpower to equally distribute patrol time and increase interaction with the community. Even though the patrol workload was analyzed twice a year and reconfigured as needed, the report described an uneven distribution of patrol resources. As a result of the shift scheduling, some officers had very little uncommitted time, while others had large blocks of uncommitted time. Deployment is now based on the report's recommendation that no more than 40 percent of an officer's time be devoted to handling calls for service. Officers were previously assigned to the same general service area; however, these assignments were not permanent. In its revamping, the department ensured that officers could more readily interact with residents by remaining in permanent geographical assignments.

The report's third recommendation was that the department institute COP, as related to the recommendation for permanent area assignments. The report stated that there was no well-established interaction or communication between the police and citizens. COP was intended to directly address the need for officers to interact more with the residents in the areas they patrolled. This departmentwide philosophy emphasized that the police and citizens are co-producers of safety and order, and that they must mutually identify and resolve community problems.

The report's fourth recommendation was that the department institute POP. The report stated that the department was an incident-driven, reactive service provider. POP was described as a departmentwide, proactive approach to patrol operations in which officers identify, analyze and respond to specific community problems. This problem-solving approach was intended to address the underlying circumstances that caused crime, whereas COP was intended to create programs and an environment that increases interaction, communication and understanding between police and citizens.

The report's fifth recommendation was that the department establish a differential response system. The report highlighted a problem with the way calls for service were handled. Officers were sent immediately to every call received, even though only 19 percent could be classified as emergencies requiring immediate mobile response. There was no prioritization or management of the service workload. The recommended police response was a deliberate stacking of nonemergency calls so as not to occupy too many officers at once. A telephone reporting unit was also established to handle many reports by telephone, such as those regarding lost property, missing persons and threatening telephone calls. The department initiated a media campaign to explain telephone reporting. The department stressed that this program would keep more officers available for emergency response and give the officers larger blocks of time to conduct proactive patrol. By 1993, the telephone reporting unit was handling between 9 and 17 percent of calls for service.

The report's final recommendation was that the department improve its analytical capabilities. This was seen as necessary for basing deployment and tactics on accurate and timely information. Response times and dispatch services were also targets for improvement. The study revealed that the computer-aided dispatch (CAD) system and the records management system (RMS) were not compatible. The department subsequently hired a planning and research director to oversee data management efforts, and by 1993, integration of the CAD/RMS system was under way.

The Savannah Police Department implemented these six recommendations immediately. As a result of the recommendations, $2.6 million was budgeted to the department to fund 34 new sworn positions, vehicles and equipment, and five telephone report-takers. The department's structure was decentralized into a precinct system. Fixed geographical beats were designed to increase officers' familiarity with citizens and community problems. Using a differential police response balanced the workload and freed up officers' time.

THE SAVANNAH POLICE DEPARTMENT

The Savannah Police Department employs 517 people, including 386 sworn personnel. The department is striving to be demographically balanced and had made progress in achieving racial balance in most ranks. The number of women had increased throughout the ranks, but they are still underrepresented.

At the time of this writing, there were 154 officers, including 71 white men, 62 black men, 10 white women, and seven black women. There were 136 corporals, including 77 white men, 41 black men, eight white women, and six black women. Sergeants were predominantly white men. Of the 44 sergeants, 30 were white men, 11 were black men, one was a white woman, and one was a black woman. There were 16 lieutenants: eight white men, five black men, two white women, and one black woman. There were no women above the rank of lieutenant. There were six captains: three white men and three black men. Of the four majors, two were white men and two were black men.

Each major commands one of four department bureaus: patrol, investigations, special operations, or management services. Captains are assigned as precinct commanders in the patrol bureau or as assistant bureau commanders in investigations and management services. Command, management services, investigations, and special operations personnel are all deployed from a central police headquarters. All other personnel are assigned and deployed from their precincts.

Patrol officers are assigned to one of three eight-hour shifts. The first and third shifts rotate each month. The second shift is a permanent assignment. Officers are rarely moved from one precinct to another, and they are assigned to the same geographical service areas within precincts as much as possible.

Two units work directly for the police chief: media relations and internal affairs. The media relations unit is staffed with a civilian public information officer who informs the local media about special programs under way and is also the contact for special events or cases of interest. The internal affairs unit is supervised by a lieutenant, who reports that the police chief "takes [complaints] very seriously. The chief will set up a hearing board in a minute."

DEPARTMENTAL LEADERSHIP

The police department's top administrator is the chief, David M. Gellatly. He has held this position for over 13 years. Gellatly had some 10 years of experience as chief at other police departments before joining Savannah's force. Before becoming chief in Savannah, Gellatly was chief in Addison, Ill., for six years. His résumé lists several accomplishments since he became Savannah's chief, including getting the department national accreditation in 1989 and reaccreditation in 1993, implementing COP/POP and updating promotional procedures by using assessment centers at all levels. His subordinates describe him as a strong, decisive leader who makes it clear where he stands on issues. He is quick to point out that he hires and fires all employees. He personally interviews all new officers, and he also controls all promotions. Such an active role with these administrative responsibilities provides him with a unique opportunity to reward and punish employees for their behavior.

"The advantage of being chief in Savannah [as opposed to other cities] is that you can say, 'We're going to do this,' and there aren't too many hurdles," said Gellatly. There is no labor union to consider, and he reports that the city manager effectively shields the police department from the vagaries of local politics.

Gellatly has a reputation as a hands-on manager. "While I can be a dictator if I want to, I know where the talent is in the department," he said. He feels he provides autonomy to his personnel but also holds them accountable for results.

Gellatly says the implementation of COP/POP played a big part in the 11 percent decrease in violent crime during 1992. He is very supportive of all the community-based programs and makes his support known. Personnel throughout the agency were extremely aware of his commitment to the COP/POP initiatives and of the importance he attached to these efforts.

A key figure in the implementation of COP/POP has been Maj. Dan Reynolds, who commanded the management services division. He is the coordinator of the COP/POP initiatives and was appointed by the chief as the COP/POP "czar." In the Savannah Police Department, the czar position is an informal but recognizable position the chief creates to focus attention on certain programs or coordinate the department's efforts in solving problems, such as a pattern of street robberies. The czar designation effectively assures department personnel that the person is serving as the chief's emissary and has his full support.

Under Reynolds' guidance, the department developed a comprehensive training program in COP/POP and established processes to review and track POP projects. Reynolds heads a steering committee that discusses projects and distributes information throughout the department. As head of the department's management services, Reynolds also coordinated several aspects of COP, such as the development of standard operating procedures. Many in the department describe Reynolds as the driving force behind COP/POP and its biggest "cheerleader."

PROBLEM-ORIENTED POLICING IN SAVANNAH

Problem-oriented policing or problem solving is a cornerstone of COP in Savannah. Although structured as separate approaches to policing, *COP* and *POP* are terms used interchangeably by many officers, police managers and citizens. Some view the efforts as a single approach, while others see distinct differences.

The department's 1991 annual report states the following:

> Problem-Oriented Policing (POP) is so closely related to COP that, in order for either to be successful, the two must be considered effectively inseparable. POP strategies employ law enforcement as well as community resources to attack the problems [that] not only breed crime, but [also] contribute to other common annoyances [that] generate dissatisfaction in the community. This "proactive" police stance eliminates, or at least mitigates, these conditions before they develop into incidents requiring police response. . . .

> Community-Oriented Policing removes the barriers that have traditionally existed between law enforcement and the public. By acquainting the police with the people they serve and, as a result, acquainting the public with individual officers, citizens no longer view police as nameless blue uniforms.

The department's patrol bureau commander, Maj. William L.D. Lyght Jr., summed up the different views: "COP is the philosophy; POP is a strategy. This strategy is used throughout the department and starts with the initiation of a POP project."

POP projects are documented problem-solving efforts. A formal process for addressing a problem is set forth in a standard operating procedure. A project starts with the submission of a project proposal, through the chain of command, by an officer or other employee who has identified a problem. Personnel follow the chain of command to eliminate duplication of effort, facilitate cooperation between involved units, and ensure that projects are not started for minor matters that can be resolved by other means.

Reynolds serves as the chairman of a POP steering committee composed of representatives from all ranks and from all bureaus and precincts. Monthly meetings are held to discuss active or pending POP projects. Information shared at the meetings is later shared with other department personnel; similarly, published meeting minutes are used to distribute information about POP throughout the department. POP projects are also discussed at weekly staff meetings, attended by all command and management personnel. Officers and detectives are given the opportunity to present their projects to staff to provide information and receive recognition. Gellatly acknowledges the officers for their efforts. Periodic status reports are required from the officers or special unit working on a project. These status reports are incorporated into the monthly and quarterly reports the precinct or division commanders submit to the bureau commanders and chief. Some of this information may also be periodically provided to the city manager.

Project proposals and procedures follow a standardized problem-solving process of identifying and analyzing specific problems, developing tailored responses and measuring the effectiveness of results. Any employee can initiate a POP project. Usually, an officer or detective who has noted a continuing or recurring problem initiates a project. The problem need not be a specific crime. For example, several projects have involved neighborhood conditions that affect residents' quality of life. Other problems have involved procedures that need improvement, such as the development of a medical protocol for handling child abuse victims. Officers who initiate projects are encouraged to make the contacts with other agencies or resources necessary to complete the project. The supervisors' role is to facilitate this process, if necessary.

COMMUNITY-ORIENTED POLICING IN SAVANNAH

Community-oriented policing was implemented in Savannah to address the need for the police department and community to frequently interact and work closely together to solve mutual problems. COP was intended to establish an underlying philosophy and value system that emphasize the importance of the community. The community policing values echoed the ministations' and assigned personnel's stated goals—to place police in closer proximity to the community and maximize police visibility, communications and interaction.

The most significant organizational change the department made when implementing community policing was the establishment of the precinct system. Each precinct has a substation. Any type of fixed beat or service area system would probably have addressed the geographical accountability problem the crime control study highlighted. According to Capt. Stephen Smith, the department's accreditation manager, the precinct system was developed to put the police and community together and to give the captains "ownership" of their part of the city.

Each precinct is commanded by a captain, who has a great deal of latitude to deploy resources according to identified needs. Maj. Lyght, patrol commander, pointed out that there is a great deal of responsibility along with this freedom. He and the chief hold each captain accountable for results. Captains report that the precinct system truly made them police managers. They have to be more actively involved in long-range planning and in developing support systems in the community.

Within each precinct, operational practices varied and were adapted to meet the area's specific needs. A few custom forms, such as daily activity reports, were used, and some precincts produced analysis and statistical reports specific to their areas. Each precinct had an administrative officer who compiled crime information for patrol officers to review. The precinct lieutenants and sergeants also used this information to determine deployment needs and special tactics. Any information on trends was shared at shift briefings and posted on bulletin boards.

The 1st Precinct was commanded by Capt. Ralph M. Bashlor Jr. and was a prototype for the department's COP/POP effort. This precinct is responsible for providing police services to the historical and downtown district, where the majority of the tourist attractions are located. Bashlor was very supportive of COP/POP. This support was evident in an article he wrote for a local newspaper in December 1992, describing COP as "something exciting happening at the Savannah Police Department" and reporting "a level of energy being generated by both the new officers and the seasoned veterans, a level of excitement unequaled in years past."

The 1st Precinct has a full-time bicycle patrol unit. The unit is used extensively to patrol the historic and waterfront areas that are the city's main tourist attractions. Many daytime workers also shop and dine in the area.

Citizens most frequently complained about panhandling and public drinking by homeless men, who were often aggressive and belligerent. Recently, one corporal started a POP project to address this ongoing problem. The entire bicycle unit worked on the project, which began when officers conducted a survey of citizens who worked in the area and of their customers. The survey asked what the most serious problems were and how the police could be most effective. The bicycle unit was deployed on a split shift that covered the times suggested in the survey responses.

The project had an immediate impact. The bicycle officers made frequent contacts with the transients and arrested several of them, quickly reducing the number of transients who loitered in the area. The officers then conducted a second survey to measure the project's impact. Citizens reported that conditions had improved significantly since the project had begun, although they also requested the continued presence of the bicycle unit. The officers also held a public meeting to share the results of the high-visibility project and of the follow-up survey. This ensured that area citizens were aware of the police's responsiveness and of the tactics' effectiveness. The officers took this opportunity to exchange information with citizens and to explain the operation, reflecting the overall community-based policing philosophy.

Another example of COP in the 1st Precinct was its "Park, Walk and Talk" initiative. To carry out COP, officers are required to get out of their patrol cars and conduct 30-minute foot patrols at least twice a shift. These foot patrols are not directed patrols intended to address specific crime problems. Rather, they are intended to establish a relationship between officers and the people who live and work in the area. Officers are encouraged to make as many citizen contacts as possible, especially with business owners and residents, to get to know them on a personal, cooperative level. Officers are also required to attend any community meetings that are held during their shift. The precinct maintains a monthly schedule of all such meetings. The department planned to expand the "Park, Walk and Talk" program to all precincts as a core part of its COP effort.

In contrast to the 1st Precinct, the 2nd Precinct is still in the early stages of implementing COP/POP. The precinct experimented with using a POP team to address community problems. One officer from each shift was assigned to work on a group approach. According to the precinct's lieutenant, the team approach prevented many officers from gaining experience in problem solving. To correct this problem, there were tentative plans to rotate the POP team assignment every three months to expose more officers to problem solving; however, during 1993, the POP team was temporarily suspended due to an unusually heavy workload. The lieutenant said many officers did not really understand the program, were unaware of available resources and were too busy on calls for service to work on POP projects.

The 2nd Precinct is the busiest area of the city in terms of calls for service and crime problems, and officers spend much of their time handling calls for service. A bicycle unit is infrequently deployed on an as-needed basis. The 2nd Precinct also has "Park, Walk and Talk," but, according to the lieutenant, "this fizzles out when calls increase." He reported that officers try to spend a little extra time on their calls and "get to know the people."

Thus, there are distinctions in the level of problem solving that occurs in patrol. However, captains' monthly reports to the patrol major highlight POP projects undertaken and progress made, as well as community organization efforts (such as Neighborhood Watch) and crime prevention initiatives. It is noteworthy that these reports also detail time lost due to injuries on duty, sick leave taken, overtime and compensatory time used, personnel and vehicle inspections made, numbers of specific types of arrests made, and crimes that occurred in the precinct.

Despite the emphasis on proactive approaches, the Savannah Police Department is still highly traditional. For example, there was much excitement in early 1993 about the department's acquisition and distribution of Glock .45-caliber pistols. Most daily activity reports still track standard law enforcement measures such as arrests.

How much problem solving has occurred in the department? Although much of the problem solving may in fact occur informally, without officers' using forms or the formal process, during 1992, the department logged 43 POP projects. These projects addressed such problems as drug dealing, false alarms, prostitution, and Sunday liquor sales. By 1993, many of the 1992 projects were reported as completed. However, a number of projects—14—were canceled for various reasons.

ORGANIZATIONAL SUPPORT FOR COMMUNITY POLICING

Despite what might seem to be an uneven implementation of COP/POP in the Savannah Police Department, the agency has been heavily involved in developing organizational support structures to systematically expand the concept. For example, the department has emphasized integrating the COP/POP concept into other units, ranging from communications to crime prevention, from tactical to traffic.

In its decentralized delivery of police service, each precinct has a crime prevention officer assigned by the special operations division. These officers analyze all crime reports as they are processed through the precinct. They produce spot maps for officers to use, and they also produce a report that recaps crimes for the past three days. This effort ensures that useful and timely information is available to the patrol officers.

The special operations bureau is heavily involved in COP/POP. This bureau includes the traffic unit and the tactical reaction and prevention (TRAP) unit, a special-mission and antidrug unit. Both these units routinely use POP techniques. This is especially true in the traffic unit's work on reducing accidents. The traffic and TRAP units are often involved in helping the precincts with problem areas. The TRAP unit may be used for any POP project that involves a large commitment of personnel or a plainclothes, tactical approach.

Training

The department has developed an extensive training program for COP/POP that is much more than simply an introduction to the philosophy and procedures. In the planning stages of the COP/POP implementation, a comprehensive review of the two initiatives was conducted to determine what skills and knowledge officers would need to perform well in COP and to carry out POP projects. Based on the review, eight independent training modules were developed and personnel training was initiated. All sworn and nonsworn personnel were included in the training. The training was launched in a developmental manner so that modules may be changed as additional training needs are identified.

In addition to the main concepts of COP and problem solving, a variety of other topics are presented. For personal and professional development, there is training in participatory decision-making and leadership. To improve officers' ability to better relate with citizens, there is training in improving communications skills and organizing citizens groups. Officers are informed of resources in the community and in other public agencies during training in referral systems. A POP training manual guides instruction.

The total training program lasts about four days for supervisors and three days for officers. Modules usually last four hours. One module for supervisors lasts six hours. Each precinct schedules its own training, but personnel are required to complete at least one module quarterly. Training was well under way in 1993.

Evaluation

In 1993, Savannah police officers were being evaluated on their problem-solving activities, although there was still significant consideration of more traditional performance indicators, such as arrest statistics. An officer productive in traditional performance areas would still receive excellent evaluations. However, supervisors were beginning to place more emphasis on involvement in COP/POP. Supervisors were also beginning to recognize that officers heavily involved in these efforts would not produce easily quantifiable work products.

Promotion and Recognition

Involvement in COP/POP, while not a prerequisite, may improve officers' chances for promotion. A recently promoted sergeant, Richard Zapal of the 2nd Precinct, was sure his work on POP projects and interaction with the community helped earn him his promotion. As a patrol officer, he personally delivered to residents in his assigned area a letter in which he introduced himself and provided his work schedule and phone number.

According to Reynolds, the emphasis on COP/POP involvement in evaluation and promotion is intended to help institutionalize community policing and problem solving within the department. This consideration and the extensive training program are important steps toward this goal.

Officers who develop projects are recognized at staff meetings and in department publications such as the training and information bulletin, published bimonthly.

Forms

The department had developed and used a number of standardized forms to track COP/POP efforts. For example, there is a form that formalizes a request to open a POP file. This form establishes a problem identification number and provides guidance regarding agencies from which to obtain information or assistance.

The department also uses a POP tracking form, which tracks the start and completion dates of the phases of the problem-solving model. Patrol captains' monthly reports to the patrol major include the status of COP strategies, status of POP, information about community interactions, and other related information.

Planning

Consistent with the city manager's background in planning, the police department routinely engages in strategic planning for the future. The department develops formal goals as part of the city's planning process. For 1993, many of these goals were related to COP/POP—some were broadly related, while others were related to specific crime problems. These were developed departmentwide, by bureaus, units and patrol precincts. Many of the patrol goals related to reducing serious community problems in specific service areas (for example, reducing commercial robberies and false alarms in Service Area 1). The horse patrol wanted to reduce thefts from vehicles, street robberies and purse snatches in the historic district by 10 percent during on-duty hours. Despite the department's commitment to COP/POP, however, many of the standards relate to achieving the ends of problem solving (for example, "increasing the number of arrests for prostitution" instead of the incidence of prostitution).

COMMUNITY OUTREACH AND COLLABORATION

In addition to developing internal mechanisms to support COP/POP, the police department has invested time and effort to build a supportive external environment for its proactive response. One example of this external investment has been the agency's launching of a citizens academy.

Citizens Academy

The department started a citizens academy to give citizens an inside look at the practices of law enforcement in general and of the Savannah Police Department in particular. The academy meets for three hours a week for 10 weeks. All of the department's functional areas, such as patrol, communications and investigations, are discussed and explained through lectures or demonstrations. Other topics include high-liability areas and COP. The academy also includes a ride-along of at least four hours.

The first class was held in February 1993 and included a cross-section of the community, men and women of all ages, business owners and those interested in a law enforcement career. Although any citizen can attend, the police department has targeted community leaders. Over time, the academy is expected to help citizens develop a greater understanding of police resources and limitations and improve the department's relationship with the community.

Volunteer Program

The Savannah Police Department has an extensive volunteer program that was established in 1992 as a means to improve service delivery without increasing costs, using citizen volunteers to supplement police resources. In 1993, the department had 42 volunteers, ranging from young adults to the elderly. Volunteers engage in a variety of assignments, such as taking vehicles to and from service stations, answering questions at the information desk or helping detectives with call-back work. As they have gained experience and acceptance, their duties have been expanded.

Volunteers receive training and also learn about the basic philosophy of COP and POP. Most of the volunteers have developed a good understanding of COP and have learned much about the department. "They know that the police want to improve the overall quality of life in Savannah—not alone, but as partners with the community," said the volunteer coordinator.

The department's outreach efforts create an opportunity for department members to interact and communicate with a wide spectrum of the community. In addition, there are many other means by which this involvement takes place. Department members are involved in a variety of committees and task forces throughout the city. The chief encourages this involvement. These groups deal with issues ranging from dilapidated housing to artwork for the city.

One important group in which police have been active is the Savannah Crime Control Collaborative (known as the Collaborative). The Collaborative's mandate is to effect changes in the policies, procedures and funding patterns of community institutions in Savannah and Chatham County to free the area of crime, juvenile delinquency and drug abuse and addiction.

The Collaborative addresses crime from a multidisciplinary perspective. Its 38 members come from local law enforcement, criminal justice, social services, education, health services, and religious organizations, as well as other civic and professional organizations. The Collaborative has a special law enforcement committee that addresses issues specific to the police. The Collaborative monitors programs and funding and makes recommendations to coordinate efforts and increase interagency problem solving. Savannah Police Department members, including the chief, are actively involved in the Collaborative. Though many citizens want more police officers or at least more police visibility, the Collaborative tries to determine whether the police department is using its officers in the best possible way.

THE FUTURE OF COP/POP

The department has several goals for expanding COP/POP in the future. One goal is to have all precincts involved in the programs at a relatively equal level. While it is acknowledged that there will always be differences between precincts, a more consistent approach is desired.

Perhaps this growth of COP/POP throughout the department will make the distinctions between the two programs clearer to officers and other staff. Many could not articulate a difference between COP and POP.

It is clear that the Savannah Police Department is working hard to have a successful community-based policing program. The department has demonstrated concern for the community through the community-based programs already in place, and it has experienced some success. With progressive leadership, the department was already involved in some community-oriented programs. With the completion of the department's restructuring and with the initiation of POP training and other implementation activities, the department has completed its first experimental stage and "learned a lot." Although the department had conducted no formal evaluation of the COP/POP efforts at the time of this writing, it planned to reevaluate its implementation and make any needed modification.

Regardless of the political nature of the original motivation to implement COP/POP, the Savannah Police Department has seized the opportunity. Additional funding and staff have enabled the department to make progress in becoming a community-oriented agency and to move forward in its problem-solving efforts.

Appendix

Case Study Protocol

The following protocol should be used as a guide for gathering the type of information needed for this project. The questions deal with the context and background events that stimulated the need for community policing strategies in the department, as well as the implementation of community policing itself. Answers to these questions will chronicle the development of community policing, the decisions made and the response(s) implemented.

The Environment

- What are the jurisdiction's economic conditions (e.g., median income, unemployment rate, poverty rate, revenue of the city over the past five years, and budget history for the police department)?

- What are the jurisdiction's demographic characteristics, population changes (size and demographic) and other background factors?

- What is the scope and nature of the current crime problem? What reoccurring crime problems are of primary concern? How has the call load changed in recent years?

- What is the city's form of government (city manager vs. strong mayor)? What is the relationship between key elected officials and the chief of police? What type of political arrangements are there? To what degree are departmental responses influenced by local politics?

- What is the political atmosphere? Single districts vs. multi-districts? What are the goals of the city council/mayor? Were key officials elected on a crime platform or other factors that affect police operations?

- What types of community organizations are there? Are there neighborhood groups? How active is the community in policing? How high is the fear factor?

- Is there cooperation from the community? Are they supportive of community-oriented policing work? Has the department's relationship with the community changed over time?

The Department

Background

- What is the department's culture (e.g., chief's tenure and management style; recurrent problems within the department, such as union issues, pay issues or racial conflict; recurrent problems within the community, such as racial conflict or excessive-force issues; internal and external political/social environment)? What are the changing demographics of the department (race/ethnicity)?

- What is the department's organizational structure, staffing and resource allocation plan? Has the department flattened its organizational structure? How? Has the department grown or lost personnel in recent years?

- Who are key decision-makers in the organization? What is their tenure and experience?

Community Policing: Planning

- Why did the department make the decision to develop a community policing program? How was the decision made? What historical events preceded the decision to implement community policing? Was there a key event that led to community policing being implemented?

- Who have been the major opponents, advocates and/or change agents for community policing, both inside and outside the department? What did they do? How involved were officers in the decision-making process?

- What terminology does the department use for their community policing program? What is/was the mission statement? What is the focus? Has it changed?

- What is the department's definition of community policing? How is the definition reflected in policies and procedures? Has the department's definition of community policing changed? How? Have all the department's policies and procedures been reviewed/modified to be consistent with community policing?

- Prior to community policing, how did the department respond to problems? What related programs existed? What factors were most important to the department in addressing problems (e.g., response time)?

- Where did the funds come from to implement community policing? What was the funding strategy?

- What was the department's strategy for implementation of community policing? Are the results immediate or long-term? Have long-term plans been developed?

Community Policing: Implementation

- Is the department's community policing effort implemented on a departmentwide basis, or is it restricted to special unit(s)? If so, how is the unit structured? How is it staffed? How does the unit interact with the other units/members of the department? How is it decided who will partake in community policing efforts?

- How is personnel performance measured? Has it changed? Has the promotional process changed? Are promotional candidates tested on community policing material?

- How are officers selected and trained for specialist community policing assignments? Are outside consultants used? Has the department sent officers to other sites?

- How much community policing training has been conducted, and in what form (academy, in-service, roll call, other)? Any specialized training such as cultural awareness, how to work with citizens, etc.?

- What type of training materials and curricula were used for implementation? How was community policing integrated into the training curricula? Are both specialists and line officers trained? The same or differently?

- What percentage of time do police officers spend on preventive patrol? How much of an officer's time is uncommitted? Do officers complete activity logs? Is uncommitted time analyzed?

- What is the shift schedule? What type of rotation plans are used? Are patrol officers assigned to fixed beats? Has the schedule changed since community policing was implemented?

- Does the department have a differential response to calls—delayed response, telephone reporting, etc.? How long has this been in place? How have call loads changed in recent years? Why?

- Is there an incentive program for the officers, such as informal/formal rewards and recognition? What informal rewards are used? What types of activities does formal recognition award?

- Does the accreditation process affect problem-solving efforts? How?

Management of Community Policing

- What is the management process? How are community policing efforts approved? What is the role of the supervisor? Is there autonomy?

- How is information about community policing communicated within the department? Does the department use newsletters, bulletin boards, memoranda, meetings, roll call, etc., to communicate?

- What do specialist and generalist officers do now that they did not do before the community policing effort? Are officers doing what they are supposed to? Are there measures/controls to [e]nsure accountability?

- Are officers assigned specific problems to address, or are they allowed to select them? Does the department routinely analyze problems, such as conducting repeat call analysis?

- Do officers collaborate with members of special units (gangs, narcotics, etc.) or divisions (crime analysis, etc.) within the department? How often? How does this collaboration occur? Does the department have a community relations unit? If so, how is it differential from community policing, and how does collaboration occur?

- Is there a central file of problem-solving/community policing efforts? Who contributes to the file? Who has access to information?

- Can individuals at levels from chief to officer give a description of how officers are supposed to behave under community policing?

- Can these same individuals give valid examples of community engagement or problem solving? Mutually supporting, or contradictory? Can they describe the underlying dynamic of problems, with evidence from multiple sources?

- When successes are described, is there evidence to support the assertion? What are the strengths and weaknesses of the community policing program?

- What barriers were encountered in implementation? How were the barriers overcome? What barriers still exist, and what are the plans to overcome them?

- What were the initial criteria developed to measure the effectiveness of community policing officers? How are officers monitored? Is there much feedback on solutions and resources? Are records kept of problem-solving efforts?

External Collaboration

Media

- What is the relationship between the media and the department? Were [the media] educated about community policing? Do reporters have free access in the department? Are officers allowed to talk with reporters?

- Were any activities conducted to gain support for the community policing program, such as training of community groups, developing of marketing pieces, etc.?

- Does the department disseminate information about community policing successes to the media? How, and how often?

Community

- How does the department respond to a community crisis? How mobile are the community police officers? How accessible are the police to the community?

- How dependent/independent is the community on/[from] the police department? What type of long-term commitments are there from the police?

- When describing problems or problem solving, are officers able to name community members and/or local government agents with whom they have worked? How do they look for or obtain alliances within the community?

- How do police officers interact with the community? Do they attend community meetings, follow up with citizens, handle phone calls, etc.?

Other Agencies

- Did the department conduct training or briefing sessions for personnel of other agencies to teach them about community policing?

- Does the department have a mechanism for interagency collaboration? Do officers contact agencies directly? What is the level of cooperation? Does the department have a resource guide or other mechanism to provide officers with information about other agencies?

- With what other agencies does the department collaborate in its community policing efforts?

- What interagency links exist for the community policing effort? (Draw organizational chart showing linkages.) Are these linkages formal or informal? What individuals participate in the interagency collaboration?

Results or Outcomes

- What has been the outcome of the department's community policing efforts? What attitudes do department members have towards the way in which community policing efforts are conducted? How do department members perceive the attitudes of the community towards community policing efforts?

- In retrospect, what other approaches to community policing could have been used?

- What is the impact of the community policing effort as revealed by department members, articles, reports, and statistics? Has there been any evaluation of effectiveness of the community policing effort? If so, what were the results?

- What were the initial goals, objectives and tasks, and did the department achieve them? Were the initial goals changed? Why? How? By whom? How did the department measure their success of community policing?

- What are the department's plans for the future, as related to community policing?

Information needed from each site:

- organizational chart and job descriptions

- annual reports (including crime data) from before the implementation of community policing to the present

- copies of special/daily training bulletins and reports relative to community policing, including news releases from the public information officer

- copy of standard operating procedure for community policing effort, including policies, procedures, directives, etc.

- mission statement

- newspaper articles

- community policing curricula and academy curricula

- performance appraisal form

- promotional process (including reading list)

- any community policing or problem-solving forms

- copies of resource guides

ABOUT THE POLICE EXECUTIVE RESEARCH FORUM (PERF)

The Police Executive Research Forum (PERF) is a national professional association of chief executives of large city, county and state law enforcement agencies. PERF's objective is to improve the delivery of police services and the effectiveness of crime control through several means:

1. the exercise of strong national leadership,

2. the public debate of police and criminal justice issues,

3. the development of research and policy, and

4. the provision of vital management leadership services to police agencies.

PERF members are selected on the basis of their commitment to PERF's objectives and principles. PERF operates under the following tenets:

1. Research, experimentation and exchange of ideas through public discussion and debate are paths for the development of a comprehensive body of knowledge about policing.

2. Substantial and purposeful academic study is a prerequisite for acquiring, understanding and adding to that body of knowledge.

3. Maintenance of the highest standards of ethics and integrity is imperative in the improvement of policing.

4. The police must, within the limits of the law, be responsible and accountable to citizens as the ultimate source of police authority.

5. The principles embodied in the Constitution are the foundation of policing.